PUPPET SCRIPTS
FOR CHILDREN'S
CHURCH

JESSIE P. SULLIVAN

BAKER BOOK HOUSE
Grand Rapids, Michigan

First printing, February 1978
Second printing, September 1978
Third printing, March 1980
Fourth printing, January 1981
Fifth printing, July 1982
Sixth printing, December 1983
Seventh printing, July 1985
Eighth printing, March 1987

CONTENTS

INTRODUCTION

My grandson, Michael, who is almost seven, was visiting my house with his two-year-old sister, Holly. Before the children had arrived, I had set up a puppet stage in my front room with the Mortimer and Mathilda marionettes prepared to perform. I had lined up chairs in front of the stage, ready for the audience.

When they arrived, Michael and Holly were both excited about the puppet show. I must admit that Holly had to be reminded by her mother several times to sit still, but Michael sat intrigued during the entire performance.

This was my first experience with marionettes, which I had just purchased for only $5.50 each; and I was trying them out on my grandchildren. I held Mathilda in one hand and Mortimer in the other, moving each marionette as its voice played on the prerecorded tape I had made.

After the show, Holly and Michael made a beeline for the marionettes behind the stage. But I remembered that one of the most important things about puppeteering is not to allow the boys and girls to see or play with the puppets at any time, so I quickly packed Mortimer and Mathilda before the children could get to them.

I got to thinking about it later and, indulgent grandmother that I am, I invited Michael over alone the next day to do a show with me. He was fantastic. He took the job very seriously as he operated Mortimer. I worked Mathilda.

Very carefully he manuevered Mortimer's legs and arms in time to the voice coming over the recorder. I couldn't see why he couldn't help me in an actual performance.

But where? We don't go to the same church, and besides, I knew it wouldn't be a good idea to let a child get involved with the puppeteering in our group. Everybody would want to be in on the act!

So, Michael and I made arrangements to give the show on a Sunday evening for the group of children at his church. It was one of the warmest experiences of my life.

The children were ecstatic when they saw the puppet stage. Although they came in excited and noisy, they soon were seated in front of the stage. Some sat on chairs, but most of them were sitting on tables and on the floor.

While my husband introduced the show, telling the children to listen carefully so they could tell him later what the puppet show was about, Michael and I prayed together behind the stage and got ready to let Mortimer and Mathilda down onto the platform.

The show began.

One of the frustrating things about being a puppeteer is that you don't know how the audience is reacting, especially in a marionette show. You are looking down onto the stage, behind the curtain. If you're using hand puppets, your stage may have a curtain that you can see through. But Michael and I couldn't see anything. In fact, we couldn't hear anything, either! It was like performing in a vacant room!

When we were about halfway through the program, however, I began to see little faces peering up at us. The children on the floor had scooted up so close they were able to see Michael and me above the marionettes! But the funny thing was that they weren't looking at Michael and me—they were looking at Mortimer and Mathilda!

Since our stage was small, I looked out around it from the side and tried to catch the attention of the teenager who was sitting at the side of the group, to ask her to have the children move back. But *she* was watching the marionettes so closely I couldn't attract her attention!

While I was trying to get her to look at me, I saw the children around her. They were enthralled, every eye on the stage.

I never did distract the children, but I was finally able to get the teenager's eye and motioned for her to move back the children who were so close to us.

I think the Lord gave me this experience for a reason. If I had ever doubted the value of puppetry, I sure can't any more. Those fidgety boys and girls I had seen before the show had been transformed.

And, to cap the whole thing off, they were able to tell my husband the meaning of the Bible verse we had been teaching. Some could even quote a little of it, though it was a very long one!

The attention of those rough and rowdy youngsters had been captured long enough for them to learn a Bible truth.

* * *

Here are some suggestions that might help you with your puppet show.

BEFORE THE SHOW

An adult should introduce the show. He might introduce the puppets, but never the puppeteers. It is a good idea to suggest that the boys and girls listen carefully so they can explain later what the puppets have talked about. Also, have the children try to learn the verse the puppets explain, if it is short and easy enough.

THE SCRIPT

All the scripts in this book are geared to teach a Bible truth and a verse. If the script is given live, the dialogue can be pinned or glued to the back of the stage so the puppeteers don't have to memorize it. However, it's much easier for the puppeteers to perform if the script has been prerecorded on tape. Besides sounding more professional, the puppeteers can give more attention to their puppets if they don't have to be thinking about saying their lines. Also, if the script is prerecorded, the voices don't have to be those of the persons manipulating the puppets. There can also be musical introductions and sound effects.

In recording the tape, you'll want to leave longer pauses between speeches than in normal conversation. Give the puppeteers an opportunity to mouth the words without being too rushed.

Also, when the scene changes, allow enough time on the tape for the puppets to do what they're supposed to do—like leave the stage, or come in.

THE PUPPETEERS

When you have only two puppets, it's possible for one person to manipulate both. This, of course, is difficult in one sense, because you have both hands to think about, but it's simpler because rehearsals can be handled at your convenience.

An ideal puppeteering group is a youth group with an adult director. If you are able to organize such a group, you can use people who don't have dramatic experience. Each person would have a definite responsibility, such as sound, puppet manipulating, costumes, or stage managing. Probably teams of four or five would work best for each skit.

THE PUPPETS

Since the puppet skits in this book are serious, and written for puppets representing people with souls and spirits, it is important to use people puppets.

Mortimer and Mathilda do not change. They retain the same characters and voices in all plays.

If a group is organized to give puppet shows, weekly rehearsals are necessary. Don't allow a sloppy performance. It takes a lot of practice to put on a good show, and it should be done for the glory of God. One very good reason for regular rehearsals is to develop strength in your hands and arms so you don't get too tired. If you are using hand puppets, you can kneel as you perform, holding your arm up straight, without bending it at the elbow. Then you won't tire so easily.

With mouth puppets, learn to synchronize the movement of the puppets's mouth with the spoken word, saving the exaggerated expressions for special times. Don't open the mouth all the way for each word. Drop the thumb on each vowel as much as possible, rather than lifting the four fingers in the upper mouth. This makes the puppet look more natural.

As one puppet speaks, you'll want to keep the other puppet motionless to avoid confusion about who is speaking. If you are using puppets with immovable mouths, this is even more important. Be sure to move only the speaking puppet, trying to move his body in time with the voice rhythm. As a puppet speaks, have him look toward the person he is addressing, and occasionally toward the audience.

THE STAGE

There are several kinds of stages which you can buy or make. Or, you can simply drape a tablecloth over the piano or hang a drape on a rod in a doorway. It all depends on how much time and energy and money you have. The height of your stage will depend upon the height of your puppeteers.

Three sides of a large cardboard refrigerator box can be used with a cut-out rectangular opening in the center for the stage. It will look something like this:

You can build a folding plywood stage on the same order, using hinges to connect the sides. It will look something like this:

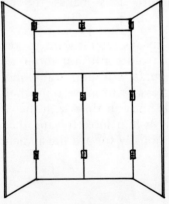

AFTER THE SHOW

As the skit finishes, the person who introduced the show should take over once more, and ask the boys and girls what they learned from the skit. This review will be helpful to all. You may also want to take time to memorize the Scripture verse or verses the puppets talked about.

When the puppet show is over, put everything away in closed containers. Do not let the children see the puppets off the stage. Keep them intact for future performances. Keep them special.

★   ★   ★

Puppets are fun for both the audience and the puppeteer! As you let Mortimer and Mathilda perform the skits in this book, they will entertain your boys and girls as well as teach them great Bible truths. God's Word is exciting, and puppets can help get that excitement across.

God bless you as you perform for His honor and His glory!

Jessie Sullivan

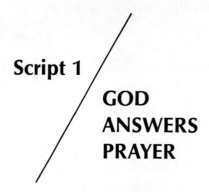

Script 1

GOD ANSWERS PRAYER

Jesus said unto him, "If thou canst believe, all things are possible to him that believeth" Mark 9:23.

(Mortimer and Mathilda enter together.)

Mortimer: *(Groans)* Oh, boy! Am I in for it! Oh, boy!

Mathilda: Why? What's the matter?

Mortimer: Oh, boy! Groan! Groan!

Mathilda: What in the world is the matter with you?

Mortimer: Oh, boy! It's caught up with me!

Mathilda: *(Exasperated)* What's caught up with you?

Mortimer: Groan. Oh, boy! I'm gonna flunk. Miss Gibson said tomorrow she's going to test us on fifty words she gave us last week to learn.

Mathilda: Last week? What's so bad about that? You've had a whole week to study them!

Mortimer: Uh. That's just it. I've tried. But they're so hard!

Mathilda: Well, it's sort of dumb of you not to study harder!

Mortimer: Dumb? Don't say that word!

Mathilda: Why haven't you studied them?

Mortimer: Well, I have. But they're so hard! And I have so much to do!

Mathilda: Like what?

Mortimer: Well, like playing basketball after school with the guys and. . . .

Mathilda: Yeah? And what?

Mortimer: Well, watching TV. . . .

Mathilda: Well, you deserve to flunk, if you ask me!

Mortimer: But that's just it! I don't *want* to flunk!

Mathilda: You should have studied more.

Mortimer: I know. But it's too late to do any more now. What'll I do?

Mathilda: Well, all I can think of is to pray and ask God to forgive you and to help you study hard tonight.

Mortimer: Do you think He'll answer a prayer like that? After all, it *is* my fault.

Mathilda: Yeah. I know. But God says He'll forgive us if we ask Him to. And He says He'll answer prayers if we believe He will. Why don't you ask Him to help you concentrate real hard so you can learn 'em better?

Mortimer: Do you think He'll answer a prayer like that? Is it in the Bible?

Mathilda: Sure. In Mark 9:23, Jesus says, "If thou canst believe, all things are possible to him that believeth."

Mortimer: If He says so, I believe it. But what shall I pray?

Mathilda: Well, first you ought to ask God to forgive you. You were wrong, you know, not to study harder.

Mortimer: Yeah, I know. I sure wish I had. 'Cause now I wouldn't have to be so worried.

Mathilda: It serves you right.

Mortimer: Well, don't rub it in. I'm sorry.

Mathilda: Okay. And what about God? If you're sorry, tell Him.

Mortimer: Okay. And how about the test? Can I pray that I'll get a good grade?

Mathilda: What do you think?

Mortimer: It's asking an awful lot.

Mathilda: I think so, too. And it's really not fair, because it's your own fault.

Mortimer: *(Discouraged)* I was hoping God would help me, if He forgave me. And I'll study ever so hard tonight!

Mathilda: That's it! That's it!

Mortimer: It is? What's it?

Mathilda: That! What you just said!

Mortimer: Did I just say something?

Mathilda: Sure! You can ask God to help you!

Mortimer: Help me what? Get a good grade?

Mathilda: No, silly. Help you study tonight to make up for not studying before. And help your mind to work so you can remember what you study!

Mortimer: Yeah! That's it!

Mathilda: Go ahead and pray. I'll pray with you!

Mortimer: Okay. You pray, too. *(Solemnly)* Dear God, I really am sorry I goofed my time away. Next time Miss Gibson gives me some words I'll get busy on them right away. And, God, would you please help me study hard tonight so I don't flunk that test tomorrow? Thank you. Amen.

Mathilda: That was a good prayer, Mortimer. Do you believe God will answer it?

Mortimer: I sure do. The Bible says He will. And I believe the Bible. I gotta go now, Mathilda. I'm going home and get busy on those words. I've gotta give God a chance to answer my prayer!

Mathilda: Bye, Mortimer. That's the right attitude. God always answers our prayers. If you start doubting that, just remember the verse I told you.

Mortimer: I will. And thanks, Mathilda. I'm glad I have a friend like you!

(Mortimer leaves stage first, Mathilda follows.)

Script 2

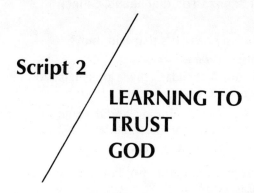

LEARNING TO TRUST GOD

Now faith is the substance of things hoped for, the evidence of things not seen Hebrews 11:1.

(Mortimer enters, whistling. Mathilda enters from opposite side of stage, gloomy.)

Mortimer: Hi, Mathilda! It's a nice day, isn't it?

Mathilda: Oh, it's okay, I guess.

Mortimer: You don't sound very okay. What's the matter?

Mathilda: Oh, nothing.

Mortimer: Well, okay. I'll be seeing you!

(Mortimer starts to go off the other side of the stage.)

Mathilda: Yeah. I'll be seeing you.

(Mortimer goes off stage. Mathilda runs after him.)

Mathilda: Hey! Mortimer! Wait a minute!

(Mortimer appears again.)

Mortimer: What? Did you call me?

Mathilda: Yes, I called you. I need your help.

Mortimer: Oh? Okay! I thought something was wrong. What's your problem?

Mathilda: Well, I don't even know if you *can* help me or not!

Mortimer: *(Getting serious)* It's that bad, huh?

Mathilda: Well it's not *bad,* but. . . .

Mortimer: Come on, Mathilda. How can I help you if you don't tell me what's wrong?

Mathilda: Well, I've been thinking about something, and I guess I just don't understand it!

Mortimer: What've you been thinking about?

Mathilda: I've been thinking about faith. I can't figure it out. Can you?

Mortimer: Well, a little. But it's hard to explain.

Mathilda: Well, that makes me feel better already. At least I don't feel so dumb. I thought I was the only one who didn't get it.

Mortimer: Oh, no. I think even a lot of grownups have trouble understanding about faith.

Mathilda: Is there a Bible verse that explains it?

Mortimer: Hebrews 11:1 helps me the most. It says, "Now faith is the substance of things hoped for, the evidence of things not seen."

Mathilda: Uh. That verse may help you, but it sure doesn't do much for me! I don't even understand the verse!

Mortimer: Well, it's like this. Most people think that faith is something way out in space, but it's really just the opposite.

Mathilda: The opposite?

Mortimer: Yeah. Faith isn't way out in the future. That's hope.

Mathilda: You mean if something hasn't happened yet, you *hope* it will happen? Is that right?

Mortimer: Right! Understand? If I *hope* for something, it means I want it to happen. It hasn't happened yet!

Mathilda: Well, I understand that all right! That's not so hard.

Mortimer: It's easier to understand faith if you understand hope.

Mathilda: I don't see any connection at all! I think you're just trying to confuse me!

Mortimer: No, I'm not. You understand what hope is. Right?

Mathilda: Right! Hope is wanting something to happen in the future.

Mortimer: Well, faith is just the opposite. Hope is wanting something *to* happen. Faith is knowing something *has already happened!*

Mathilda: Huh?

Mortimer: Hope is in the future; faith is in the present or past!

Mathilda: I don't understand.

Mortimer: If you have faith in something, you believe it has already happened! Like if you pray and ask God for something *in faith*, God has already answered your prayer!

Mathilda: But I wouldn't pray it if He'd already answered it!

Mortimer: Just because you don't *see* it doesn't mean you don't *have* it! But, besides, God wants us to pray for things.

Mathilda: Well, if I don't *see* it, I don't *have* it!

Mortimer: But as far as God is concerned, you do! If you only hope for something, it will never happen. But if you pray in faith, as soon as you ask God for something, you can thank Him for His answer!

Mathilda: I can?

Mortimer: Sure! Because as far as God is concerned, you already have it! You may not see it for a while, but it's there just the same!

Mathilda: Oh. I think I understand. I just can't *see* it yet!

Mortimer: Yeah! That's it!

Mathilda: What was that Bible verse again?

Mortimer: You mean Hebrews 11:1? "Faith is the substance of things hoped for, and the evidence of things not seen."

Mathilda: Uh-huh.

Mortimer: That's just what I've been explaining! It says faith is *substance* and *evidence*. Anything that is substance and evidence has to already be here, doesn't it?

Mathilda: Yeah. Like evidence in court. When somebody has evidence, he has something right there to prove something, doesn't he?

Mortimer: And substance is something that *exists!* It isn't something in the future. It's already here!

Mathilda: Oh, I see the difference! Hope isn't here yet, but faith is!

Mortimer: Smart girl! *(To the audience)* As if that wasn't what I was saying all the time!

Mathilda: Then when I ask God for something in faith, I should thank Him for His answer right when I ask, because as far as He is concerned, I have it already! Is that right?

Mortimer: Sure, because if you really have faith, you'll believe God.

Mathilda: Even if I don't see His answer yet!

Mortimer: But when you pray, be sure it's according to God's will. If it is, you're sure to have what you ask for.

Mathilda: Uh-oh! I knew there was a catch!

Mortimer: No catch! All you have to do is read the Bible and God tells you what His will is.

Mathilda: Oh. I see.

Mortimer: Like I know it's God's will for me to accept Jesus as my Savior!

Mathilda: Yes. I know that, too. It says so in the Bible.

Mortimer: Okay. So I can pray for Jesus to come into my heart and if I believe it, He's there! I don't see Him, but I know He's there, because God says so!

Mathilda: That's true. That's what happens, all right. I know.

Mortimer: Do you know what faith is now?

Mathilda: Yes! It's just believing what God says is true!

Mortimer: That's it! I couldn't say it better myself! When God says it, I believe it! And that settles it!

Mathilda: Wow! Thanks, Mortimer! That's fantastic! All I have to do is read the Bible and accept it just like it is. Say that's a tricky little saying. You could make a song out of that! *(Starts singing)* When God says it, I believe it! And that settles it!

(Mortimer and Mathilda both leave the stage singing the song.)

Script 3

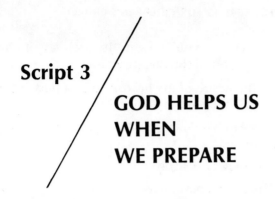

GOD HELPS US
WHEN
WE PREPARE

Go ahead and prepare for the conflict, but victory comes from God Psalm 21:31, LB.

(Mortimer is on stage. Mathilda enters, singing.)

Mathilda: La de da. La de da. I'm so happy!

Mortimer: Boy! You're so happy you're silly!

Mathilda: Well, I've been reading my Bible, and la de da I'm so happy!

Mortimer: There are a lot of things in the Bible about being happy. But I don't remember anything about being la de da happy!

Mathilda: Well, you may think I'm silly happy, but you'll be silly happy, too, when you hear!

Mortimer: Come on! Tell me! I'd like to know what sent you off so far into silly land!

Mathilda: Well, I just read in the Bible that we can ask God for the desires of our heart, and He'll give them to us!

Mortimer: Sure. There's lots in the Bible about prayer. But you have to know everything in there to be sure you know what God means!

Mathilda: But it says right in Psalms that God will do it.

Mortimer: Okay. Okay. You're right. It does say it, but what are you so silly happy about?

Mathilda: Well, the desire of my heart is to be a nurse some day! So, that verse says I will be!

Mortimer: You mean you'll be a nurse just because you *want* to be?

Mathilda: Yes, if I ask God for it.

Mortimer: Is that all you have to ask God for?

Mathilda: I guess so. . . . Isn't it?

Mortimer: Well, that's part of it all right, but God won't do it all.

Mathilda: Oh?

Mortimer: No! *You* have to do *something!*

Mathilda: Well, like go to school and stuff?

Mortimer: Right! You won't just wake up some morning with a diploma in your hand!

Mathilda: *(Quietly)* Well, I didn't expect it to happen *exactly* that way!

Mortimer: No? How did you expect it to happen?

Mathilda: Well, I guess I just expected it to be easy. Oh, not *that* easy! But easier!

Mortimer: God will help you, if it really is the desire of your heart. But, if it really *is* the desire of your heart, you'll help Him, too!

Mathilda: Why? How?

Mortimer: Well, Proverbs 21:31 talks about this. The Living Bible says, "Go ahead and prepare for the conflict, but victory comes from God."

Mathilda: You mean my getting to be a nurse is a conflict?

Mortimer: Yes, life is sort of a conflict, really. And I think nursing would be, too.

Mathilda: I think I see what you mean. You're saying that I have to do my part, and then God will do His!

Mortimer: That's right! Like He'll help us get good grades in school, but we have to study for them.

Mathilda: And He'll help us have a happy home, but we have to do our part to make it happy.

Mortimer: And He'll help us get a job, but we have to go out and look for it!

Mathilda: I think that's a good verse. I don't think we'd appreciate things if we didn't earn them.

Mortimer: I don't either.

Mathilda: And, after all, if I just woke up one morning with a nurse's diploma in my hand, it wouldn't do the patients much good! I wouldn't even know how to take care of them!

Mortimer: Hey! I don't think I'd want to be your patient, even after you go to school!

Mathilda: *(Laughs)* Oh, silly!

Mortimer: Aw. I was just kidding.

Mathilda: I think I'd like to learn that verse you told me. What was it again?

Mortimer: Proverbs 21:31. "Go ahead and prepare for the conflict, but victory comes from God."

Mathilda: Yeah, that's a good verse all right. Come on. I want to tell Mom the new verse I learned.

(Mortimer and Mathilda leave stage together.)

Script 4

GOD WANTS US TO BE UNSELFISH

Give, and it shall be given unto you; good measure, pressed down, and shaken together, and running over   Luke 6:38.

(Mortimer and Mathilda enter stage.)

Mathilda: Oh, dear. I feel miserable. Do you ever feel miserable, Mortimer?

Mortimer: Yes, I'm afraid so.

Mathilda: Do you feel miserable today?

Mortimer: No. I feel pretty good today.

Mathilda: Oh.

Mortimer: Why? Should I feel miserable today?

Mathilda: Oh, I guess not.

Mortimer: Why did you ask then?

Mathilda: Oh, I just thought if you felt miserable, too, that maybe it was because of the weather.

Mortimer: The weather? How could you blame it on the weather?

Mathilda: Well, lots of people feel like the weather! If it's sunshiny, they're sunshiny. And if it's gloomy, they're gloomy!

Mortimer: I guess that is the way a lot of people are, but I don't think that's right. We shouldn't let outside things affect us like that!

27

Mathilda: Well, I feel gloomy, and I guess it's just me.

Mortimer: That's too bad. Do you have any other reason besides the weather for feeling gloomy?

Mathilda: Yeah. I'm afraid so.

Mortimer: And you knew it all the time, didn't you?

Mathilda: Yeah, I guess so. But I didn't want to admit it.

Mortimer: What's your problem?

Mathilda: Oh, it's Ellie again.

Mortimer: Your little sister?

Mathilda: Yeah.

Mortimer: What's wrong?

Mathilda: I guess I'm not a very good big sister.

Mortimer: It's hard to be a good big sister, I bet.

Mathilda: Yeah.

Mortimer: But God will help you, if you'll let Him.

Mathilda: I know. In fact, I guess He's the one who's making me realize some things about being a good sister.

Mortimer: I wouldn't doubt it.

Mathilda: Do you know what's wrong with me?

Mortimer: No. What?

Mathilda: I'm selfish.

Mortimer: Everybody's selfish. We all want our own way all the time.

Mathilda: But that's not the way God wants us to be! I know it isn't!

Mortimer: You're right. And I remember a good verse about that. It's Luke 6:38. "Give, and it shall be given to you; good measure, pressed down, and shaken together, and running over."

Mathilda: Does that mean what it sounds like it means?

Mortimer: You know it does. If it's in the Bible, it's true!

Mathilda: But it sounds too good to be true!

Mortimer: If we'd stop to think about it, the whole Bible sounds too good to be true!

Mathilda: You're sure right there! God gives us so many things. All we have to do is to accept them! Tell me that verse again!

Mortimer: "Give, and it shall be given unto you; good measure, pressed down, and shaken together, and running over." Luke 6:38.

Mathilda: Wow! That's a good verse.

Mortimer: And there's only one word in it that tells us what we're supposed to do.

Mathilda: And all the rest is about what will happen to us if we do it! If we give, then we'll get back lots more than we give! Wow!

Mortimer: Just remember, it says in the same measure, though! Like if you give *good* things, you get *good* things back. But if you give *bad* things, you get *bad* things back.

Mathilda: I'm just going to give good things, then. In fact, I think I'll go right home and give Ellie something good!

Mortimer: It doesn't just mean *things,* I don't think. Other stuff, too, like love and understanding and, and. . . .

Mathilda: Help, and, and. . . . I'll figure something out!

(Mortimer and Mathilda leave stage.)

Voice Behind Stage: The next day.

(Mortimer and Mathilda enter.)

Mathilda: Mortimer, you'll never believe it!

Mortimer: Believe what?

Mathilda: Remember what we were talking about yesterday?

Mortimer: You mean about your being gloomy and selfish?

Mathilda: Yes! You'll never believe what happened!

Mortimer: Try me!

Mathilda: Well, I went home. And I thought and thought. I tried real hard to figure out something I could give to Ellie that was good.

Mortimer: What did you decide on?

Mathilda: Well, I couldn't decide! So I prayed!

Mortimer: That was a good idea!

Mathilda: And the minute I finished praying I thought of my doll.

Mortimer: Your doll! Do you still play with dolls?

Mathilda: Well, not much. But I have this beautiful doll that my aunt and uncle gave to me for my birthday. It's so beautiful I never play with it.

Mortimer: What use is a doll like that?

Mathilda: Well, I keep her on my bed all the time.

Mortimer: And I bet that drives Ellie wacky!

Mathilda: Right! I never thought about it like that before. I just put the doll there because that's what I wanted. I never realized what it would do to Ellie. . . . Anyway, I thought about that doll.

Mortimer: And you gave it to Ellie?

Mathilda: Well, it wasn't all that simple. Ellie's awful little, you know. And I was afraid she'd break my doll or mess her up.

Mortimer: So what did you do?

Mathilda:	I prayed again. And the more I prayed, the surer I was that that was what God wanted me to do!
Mortimer:	Did you do it?
Mathilda:	Well, Ellie knocked on my door about that time. I never let her come in unless she knocks.
Mortimer:	Come on, tell me! Did you let her have the doll or didn't you?
Mathilda:	Well, not exactly.
Mortimer:	This suspense is killing me. What happened?
Mathilda:	Well, when Ellie came in, I was still on my knees. She asked me what I was doing.
Mortimer:	Did you tell her?
Mathilda:	Yes. I just sat right there on the floor and told her I was sorry I was so selfish.
Mortimer:	What'd she do?
Mathilda:	She patted me on the cheek and said, "That's all right, Mattie, I love you!"
Mortimer:	She's awful little for that! She probably doesn't even know what selfish means.
Mathilda:	I know. I thought so, too. But I realized she wasn't as little as I'd thought.
Mortimer:	So?
Mathilda:	So, without even thinking, I asked her if she'd like to hold my doll!
Mortimer:	Yeah?
Mathilda:	Yeah. When I gave it to her, she held it very carefully. Then I asked her if she wanted to play with it.
Mortimer:	Boy! You *did* get big-hearted!
Mathilda:	But the funny thing about it was, I really meant it!

Mortimer: No kidding!

Mathilda: And do you know what Ellie did?

Mortimer: No, what?

Mathilda: She kissed my doll on the cheek and handed her back to me!

Mortimer: She gave the doll back to you?

Mathilda: Yes. And she said, "Careful. Mattie's doll." Then she watched while I put the doll back on the bed. And she just smiled and sat back on my lap.

Mortimer: After all that worrying that she'd go into your room and break your doll and all!

Mathilda: Yes. And as I hugged Ellie I suddenly realized she was much more important than any old doll.

Mortimer: I bet you didn't feel gloomy after that!

Mathilda: No, sir! I sure didn't.

Mortimer: No wonder! You really proved the verse. "Give, and it shall be given unto you; good measure, pressed down, and shaken together, and running over."

Mathilda: Thanks, Mortimer. You're a real pal. Why don't we go to my house and play with Ellie for a while?

(Mortimer and Mathilda leave stage.)

Script 5

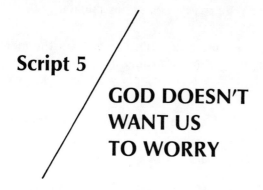

GOD DOESN'T WANT US TO WORRY

Casting all your care upon him; for he careth for you   I Peter 5:7.

(Mortimer and Mathilda enter stage together.)

Mathilda: *(Sighs)* Boy! Am I sorry I ever tried out for the play we're going to have in our class!

Mortimer: You're going to be in a play? That sounds great! Can I come and see it?

Mathilda: It might sound great to you, but it sure doesn't to me!

Mortimer: You didn't *have* to try out for a part, did you? If you didn't want to be in it, why did you?

Mathilda: I'm dumb, I guess. I didn't know it was going to be so hard. When I saw other people in plays it looked easy. I always thought it would be fun!

Mortimer: And it's not as much fun as you thought, huh?

Mathilda: It sure isn't! You have to remember so many little things. It's not just memorizing the words!

Mortimer: That would be hard enough . . . memorizing the words, I mean.

Mathilda: *(Sigh)* I thought that would be all there is to it, but wow! It sure isn't!

Mortimer: What's so hard about it?

Mathilda: Well, I'm not even doing so well on the memorizing part. But I not only have to remember the words, I have to remember what I'm supposed to be *doing*, too!

Mortimer: Oh, yeah. I guess you would have to remember that stuff!

Mathilda: Like I'm a maid in this play. See?

Mortimer: Yeah.

Mathilda: So, when I come into the room I say, "Here's your tea, Ma'am." And then I have to put it on the table.

Mortimer: That doesn't sound so hard!

Mathilda: But it is. What if I spill it? And I have to cross the room at exactly the right time and not trip over something . . . and I have to set a picture straight . . . and not knock it over. . . . And then I say, "I miss the young master."

Mortimer: That doesn't sound too hard . . . that is, if you don't trip over something or spill the tea all over the other people.

Mathilda: It sure seems hard to me. This is the first time I've ever been in a play, and I want to do it right. But like yesterday, when I straightened the picture, it fell off the hook and hit me right on the toe!

Mortimer: *(Snickering)* What'd you do?

Mathilda: I yelled. What do you think? I yelled and grabbed my toe. It hurt!

Mortimer: Oh, boy! I bet your director didn't like that!

Mathilda: You're right! He really bawled me out!

Mortimer: I guess he had to! But that won't happen when you put the play on!

Mathilda: I hope not! Because if it does, Mr. Anderson said for me to just act like nothing happened and put the picture back up on the wall!

Mortimer: You might have a comedy if you don't! That'd be funny, seeing you hopping all over the stage on one foot! *(Acts like he is hopping.)*

Mathilda: Yeah. But what's really hard is knowing what to do, and when!

Mortimer: After hearing all this, I really want to see that play!

Mathilda: *(Starts to cry)* Oh, Mortimer. I'm scared I'll mess it all up.

Mortimer: Don't say that! Hey, I know a verse for this! It's in First Peter 5:7. "Casting all your care upon him; for he careth for you."

Mathilda: Do you really think God will take care of me in the play?

Mortimer: Sure! He says He'll always take care of us, doesn't He?

Mathilda: Yes.

Mortimer: God doesn't lie, does He?

Mathilda: No.

Mortimer: Then just believe Him. Don't worry. Just give the problem to God and let Him take care of it.

Mathilda: But I have to study hard to do my part, don't I?

Mortimer: Sure. And when you get out there on that stage, if you'll let God help you, He will. No matter what happens, it's what God wants.

Mathilda: Okay. I'll work hard and memorize my part and practice and go to all the rehearsals so I'll know what to do.

Mortimer: And then, whatever happens is up to God! Just remember, He cares for you!

(Mathilda and Mortimer leave the stage.)

Mathilda: It's sure going to be hard to stop worrying. I'm so much in the habit.

Mortimer: Yeah, but you can stop. Just try.

(Mathilda and Mortimer leave the stage.)

Voice Behind Stage: It is now three weeks later. The play Mathilda was in took place last night. Mortimer and Mathilda are talking about it.

(Mortimer and Mathilda come on to stage. Mortimer is laughing. Mathilda is limping.)

Mathilda: *(Indignantly)* Well! I don't see anything so funny about it. My toe hurts! Yours would too, if a picture fell on it!

Mortimer: *(Still laughing)* Oh, Mathilda, I'm sorry your foot hurts, but I can't help it! You ought to be praising God about that part of the play!

Mathilda: Why?

Mortimer: Don't you see? If it hadn't happened during your play practice you wouldn't have known what to do when that guy knocked the picture on your foot. God helped you! If He hadn't, you'd have ruined everything if you'd yelled and danced around all over the stage on one foot!

Mathilda: *(Laughs)* Yeah. You're right. I would have ruined everything!

Mortimer: The play turned out great. I really liked it. You did a good job!

Mathilda: Well, God did a good job, really. He helped me. I couldn't have done it without Him!

Mortimer: Doesn't it feel good to know God is helping you?

Mathilda: Yeah. I'm not ever going to do anything alone again! It's silly to worry when God has promised to help me. All I have to do is let Him!

Mortimer: You and God make a good team, Mathilda!

Mathilda: Thanks to you! That was really a good verse you taught me. Let's see. "Casting all your cares upon him; for he careth for you." That's in First Peter 5:7.

Mortimer: Yeah, I think it's a good verse, too. "Casting all your cares upon him; for he careth for you." First Peter 5:7.

(Mortimer and Mathilda leave stage.)

Script 6

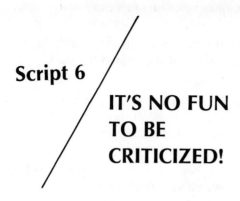

IT'S NO FUN TO BE CRITICIZED!

Judge not, that ye be not judged   Matthew 7:1.

(Mortimer and Mathilda enter. Mathilda is crying.)

Mortimer: I'm sorry you feel so bad, Mathilda.

Mathilda: *(Crying)* Oh, Mortimer, I feel awful. I feel mad and sad and embarrassed and . . . and. . . .

Mortimer: Why? What happened? You were feeling all right a little while ago.

Mathilda: *(Still crying)* Oh, Mortimer, I don't know why I feel so terrible. I know I really shouldn't, but I do.

Mortimer: Why? What happened?

Mathilda: Oh, Mortimer, I hate to tell you. It makes me feel so terrible just to think about it.

Mortimer: Maybe you'll feel better if you talk about it.

Mathilda: *(Crying)* I'll never feel better. I feel so mixed up inside. I thought Marty was my friend.

Mortimer: She is, isn't she? What makes you say she isn't?

Mathilda: Oh, after what she did to me, she can't ever be my friend again.

Mortimer: That sounds terrible! Whatever happened to make you say that?

Mathilda: She's not my friend at all. She can't be or she wouldn't talk about me behind my back!

Mortimer: What did she say?

Mathilda: She told Annie that I thought I was smart and that I wasn't smart at all, but I just acted nice to the teachers so I'd get good grades!

Mortimer: Why that's not true! I know it isn't! You get good grades because you study so hard. You deserve every good grade you ever got!

Mathilda: *(Sniffling)* Thanks, Mortimer. But it doesn't help any. I'm still mad at Marty. She shouldn't say things like that.

Mortimer: You're right. It wasn't very nice of her.

Mathilda: She's just mad because I get better grades than she does.

Mortimer: I can sure see why God says we shouldn't judge or criticize anybody. It just makes the other person feel bad. And it doesn't do us any good either.

Mathilda: You're right, Mortimer. It sure makes me feel bad to be criticized.

Mortimer: It says in Matthew 7:1, "Judge not, that ye be not judged."

Mathilda: I'm going to learn that verse. I sure don't want to hurt anybody like Marty hurt me.

Mortimer: Yes, but you still feel bad, don't you?

Mathilda: Yeah. Just knowing Marty did wrong doesn't make me feel any better.

Mortimer: I think maybe I can help you, if you want me to, Mathilda.

Mathilda: How can you help me? Nobody can ever take words back!

Mortimer: That's true, but I still think I can help you!

Mathilda: Okay. I sure need it!

Mortimer: Well, in the first place, you can't change Marty, but you can change the way you feel about her. Then you'll feel okay again!

Mathilda: I can? How?

Mortimer: Well, first, don't worry about what she said. It wasn't true, and we know it. And we know truth always comes out on top!

Mathilda: Well, I guess that part is right.

Mortimer: Don't let yourself be tempted to hate Marty for what she said, either.

Mathilda: Well, I'll try.

Mortimer: You can pray and God will help you, if you want Him to.

Mathilda: Oh. I do! I don't want to feel like this!

Mortimer: Okay. So pray and ask God to help you love Marty and to forgive her for what she did to you.

Mathilda: That's sort of hard.

Mortimer: I know. But look what the people did to Jesus, and He forgave them!

Mathilda: I want to be like Jesus.

Mortimer: Okay. So go ahead and pray. I'll pray with you.

Mathilda: Dear God, I feel bad because Marty said those things about me. Please help me to love her and to forgive her. I really don't think she meant them. And thank You for understanding. In Jesus' name I pray. Amen.

Mortimer: That was a good prayer, Mathilda.

Mathilda: Know what? I feel better already. I'm sorry Marty doesn't get good grades like I do. Maybe I could study with her and help her some time.

Mortimer: That's a great idea!

Mathilda: Thanks, Mortimer. You're smart. I'm glad you helped me. Say! What was that verse again?

Mortimer: Oh, you mean "Judge not that ye be not judged"? It's in Matthew 7:1.

Mathilda: Yes. That's the one! I think I'd better learn it, because I don't want to make anybody feel as bad as I did a while ago. They might not have you around to help them!

(Mortimer and Mathilda leave stage.)

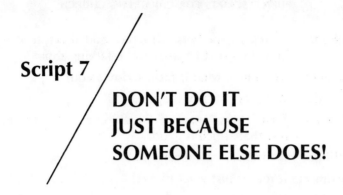

Script 7

DON'T DO IT
JUST BECAUSE
SOMEONE ELSE DOES!

Prove all things; hold fast that which is good I Thessalonians 5:21.

(Mortimer and Mathilda enter stage.)

Mathilda: Say, Mortimer, I saw you playing with Chester and Butch after school yesterday.

Mortimer: Yeah.

Mathilda: I've heard some bad things about those boys. I've even seen them smoking! You didn't smoke with them, did you?

Mortimer: Are you kidding? I know it's dumb to smoke. I can read. It's in all the papers. And cigarette manufacturers even have to put it on every package that smoking hurts you.

Mathilda: Well, most everybody our age *can* read. And Chester and Butch can read, too. But they smoke, anyway!

Mortimer: But I read the *Bible,* and they don't!

Mathilda: I guess you're right there. At least they don't go to church.

Mortimer: I learned a Bible verse about what you're talking about. It's in First Thessalonians 5:21. It's "Prove all things; hold fast that which is good."

Mathilda: That's a good verse. It's nice and short, too! But how does that fit what we're talking about?

Mortimer: You know what it means, don't you?

Mathilda: Well, sort of. Say it again.

Mortimer: First Thessalonians 5:21, "Prove all things; hold fast that which is good."

Mathilda: It means. . . . It means. . . .

Mortimer: It means just what it says!

Mathilda: Yeah. It means. . . .

Mortimer: It means that you're supposed to *prove* everything you do!

Mathilda: *(Thoughtfully)* I know how you prove an arithmetic problem!

Mortimer: You have rules to do that, don't you?

Mathilda: Yes.

Mortimer: Well, God gives us rules, too!

Mathilda: I know! In the Bible!

Mortimer: Right!

Mathilda: So?

Mortimer: Well, everything we want to do needs to be checked out by the Bible.

Mathilda: Oh!

Mortimer: And if God says it's okay, then we can do it!

Mathilda: But what if it's not?

Mortimer: That's easy. Then we don't do it!

Mathilda: Well, we were talking about smoking. There isn't anything in the Bible about smoking, is there?

Mortimer: Not that I know of. But there is a verse that says when we become Christians our bodies become the temples of God.

Mathilda: How can that be?

Mortimer: Because the Holy Spirit comes into them!

Mathilda: Yeah! That's right!

Mortimer: And, since our bodies are the temples of God, we should take care of them. Right?

Mathilda: Right!

Mortimer: And, since doctors tell us smoking isn't good for our bodies, we shouldn't smoke!

Mathilda: That's right! But what was that other verse?

Mortimer: Oh, you mean First Thessalonians 5:21? "Prove all things. . . ."

Mathilda: I see! That's proving it . . . when you check it out with the Bible!

Mortimer: Right! And the rest of the verse is "hold fast that which is good."

Mathilda: I see! If you check it out with the Bible and you find out you're not supposed to do it, you're *not* supposed to do it and. . . .

Mortimer: And if it's *right,* you're supposed to hang on to it!

Mathilda: What about Chester and Butch? Can you help them with that verse?

Mortimer: I'm afraid not. They aren't Christians. So I think what I need to do first is to tell them about Jesus. Then, when they know Him and let Him come into their hearts, they'll be able to understand the Bible better!

Mathilda: I see! And that's why you were playing with them! So they'd know you liked them and then you could tell them about Jesus!

Mortimer: Now you're getting smart!

Mathilda: Yeah. But I sure have a lot to learn!

(Mortimer and Mathilda skip off stage.)

Script 8

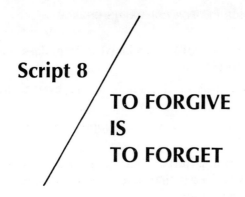

TO FORGIVE
IS
TO FORGET

And when ye stand praying, forgive, if ye have aught against any: that your Father also which is in heaven may forgive you your trespasses Mark 11:25.

(Mortimer and Mathilda enter stage.)

Mortimer: Boy! I sure feel depressed! *(Groan)*

Mathilda: Depressed? That's a new word to me. What does "depressed" mean?

Mortimer: You mean you've never been depressed?

Mathilda: How would I know? I don't even know what it means!

Mortimer: Everyone knows what "depressed" means.

Mathilda: Well, I don't. Tell me!

Mortimer: It's awful. When you feel depressed, you feel awful!

Mathilda: Well, I've felt awful before. Like when I had the measles.

Mortimer: Oh! It's not that kind of awful! It's deep down inside you!

Mathilda: Does something in particular make you feel that way?

Mortimer: I don't know. All I know is that there's this deep, dark black feeling inside me.

Mathilda: You *look* sort of like you have a deep, dark black feeling inside you.

Mortimer: I feel like nobody likes me and that everything is wrong. Oh-h-h, I feel *awful!*

Mathilda: Are you sick? Do you suppose you need a doctor?

Mortimer: Naw. Nothing hurts. That is, nothing in my body hurts. It's deeper than that. It's my feelings way down deep inside.

Mathilda: Boy! That sounds terrible!

Mortimer: Have you ever felt this way?

Mathilda: Yes. But I didn't know it was called " 'pression."

Mortimer: *(Groan) De*pression!

Mathilda: Okay. *De*pression. But there must be a reason why you feel that way. Did anybody hurt your feelings?

Mortimer: *Any*body? Just *every*body, that's all!

Mathilda: Maybe it just *seems* like everybody!

Mortimer: No. I feel like I just don't like *any*body.

Mathilda: Not even me?

Mortimer: Well, maybe I like you a *little!*

Mathilda: Wow! Mortimer! I don't like it when you feel this way! When did you first start feeling *de*pressed?

Mortimer: Oh, I don't know. I think it came on sort of gradually.

Mathilda: Well, God doesn't want us to feel depressed, I know *that.* He wants us to be happy.

Mortimer: I'd *like* to feel that way, but I sure don't!

Mathilda: Hmmm. Mortimer, do you know what I think?

Mortimer: No, what?

Mathilda: I think you should pray about it!

Mortimer: I've tried. And it seems like God doesn't even hear me.

Mathilda: If you could get rid of those bad feelings, you could be cheerful and happy like God wants you to be. Right?

Mortimer: So—what else is new?

Mathilda: Would you try an experiment with me?

Mortimer: I don't feel like trying any old experiment. I don't feel like doing *anything!*

Mathilda: But I think you'll feel better if you'll do it!

Mortimer: Well, okay. I couldn't feel any worse.

Mathilda: Well, this is what I think. The Bible says that if we want God to answer our prayers we're supposed to be forgiving. Maybe you're holding some grudges against some people. That's unforgiveness, you know.

Mortimer: Oh . . . well . . . uh . . . yeah.

Mathilda: This is my experiment. Let's go home and make a list of all the people we have something against. Then, let's come back here and pray about all those people, and forgive them!

Mortimer: I don't know! It won't be so hard to do the first part, but that second part doesn't sound so easy!

Mathilda: We only have to do one part at a time! Let's try it!

Mortimer: Okay. But I doubt if it'll work!

Mathilda: See you in an hour!

(Mortimer and Mathilda leave stage.)

Voice Back Stage: One hour later.

(Mortimer and Mathilda come back on stage. Each has a long sheet of paper pinned or scotch taped to his hand. Mortimer's sheet is much longer than Mathilda's.)

Mathilda: I see you made your list!

Mortimer: Yeah. Once I got started, I could hardly stop!

Mathilda: No wonder you felt so bad. You know that each grudge is a sin against God. And when we don't forgive somebody for something we just keep on holding that grudge.

Mortimer: You're telling me! Wow! No wonder God wouldn't answer my prayers! Just look at this list!

Mathilda: It *is* pretty long!

Mortimer: It's silly the way I've been holding things against people. They probably don't even know it, most of the things are so little. Like Billy. Do you know I don't like him because he threw the baseball too high for me to catch in a baseball game way *last summer?*

Mathilda: Boy! You did go a long way back!

Mortimer: Yeah. And Ernie didn't share a candy bar with me a couple of months ago! Isn't that silly? After all, maybe Ernie was hungry. Or maybe he just didn't think!

Mathilda: Yeah! We all do things like that sometimes!

Mortimer: And I don't like Miss Brown because she didn't give me a good grade on my exam! But it wasn't *her* fault that I didn't do better!

Mathilda: You're getting the right idea! But I had some names, too. Like Madge makes me mad because she's always complaining! But poor Madge doesn't know that God wants us to have joy.

Mortimer: You know what, Mathilda? I'd really like to ask God to forgive me for holding these grudges. And I really want Him to, too. How do I do it?

Mathilda: Well, how about reading the list off to Him and asking Him to forgive you for each grudge? I need to do that, too!

Mortimer: Okay. We can both do it at the same time because we won't have to pray out loud, will we?

Mathilda: No, because God knows everything. He knows when we're *thinking* a prayer.

(Mortimer and Mathilda pray silently.)

Voice Behind Stage: While Mortimer and Mathilda are asking God to forgive them for having bad feelings, perhaps you boys and girls in the audience would like to ask Him to forgive you, too. Mark 11:25 says that if you have anything against anybody God wants you to forgive him. Each one of you, bow your head right now. As you think of people you have something against, ask God to forgive you for holding these bad feelings. Now forgive each person for whatever you are holding against him.

(Have a brief silence.)

Voice Behind Stage: Dear God, thank You for giving us forgiving spirits. And thank You especially for being so forgiving to us. In Jesus' name we pray. Amen.

(Mortimer and Mathilda start moving again.)

Mortimer: Boy! I feel so much better! Isn't God great? He knows what makes us feel bad. That's why He tells us to do the things He does!

Mathilda: Yes. And now that we've forgiven these people, let's do what God does. Let's *forget* we ever had anything to forgive them for!

Mortimer: Great! And do you know what I'm going to do? I'm going to go home and tear my list up into little bitty shreds and throw them away! That'll be the end of all my grudges.

Mathilda: Me, too! That'll show we've not only forgiven everybody, but we've even forgotten what we were mad about!

(Mortimer and Mathilda hurry off stage.)

Script 9

THANK GOD IN EVERYTHING (Thanksgiving)

In every thing give thanks: for this is the will of God in Christ Jesus concerning you I Thessalonians 5:18.

(Mortimer enters from left side of stage. He is very sad. Mathilda enters from right side of stage.)

Mathilda: Hi, Mortimer. You look awfully sad. What's the matter?

Mortimer: Oh, everything. Everything bad has happened to me today. When I got up, I couldn't find my shoes. When I ate breakfast, I spilled my milk. And then when I left for school, I couldn't find my homework.

Mathilda: You have had a rough day, all right.

Mortimer: Yeah. It's funny. Some whole days are like that.

Mathilda: You're right. Some whole days *are* like that. But, listen—have you thanked God for all these bad things yet?

Mortimer: Thanked God? Are you kidding? Thanked God for all that bad stuff happening to me? Do you think I'm crazy?

Mathilda: No, but God tells us in First Thessalonians 5:18 that we're to thank Him for everything.

Mortimer:	That's kind of hard. But God knows everything, so what He says must be right. What's the rest of that verse?
Mathilda:	It's "In every thing give thanks: for this is the will of God in Christ Jesus concerning you."
Mortimer:	And that's in the Bible?
Mathilda:	Yes, in First Thessalonians 5:18.
Mortimer:	Boy! That's a funny verse! What does it mean? How can you thank God for all that bad stuff? I sure don't *feel* thankful!
Mathilda:	It doesn't say that we have to *feel* thankful. Just to thank God. You want to be obedient to Him, don't you?
Mortimer:	Sure, but that's not so easy. What does it mean, anyway?
Mathilda:	Just what it says. God knows all about us and He knows everything that happens to us, so He has a purpose in mind when He allows something bad to happen to us. It seems funny, but He does. And He wants us to trust Him.
Mortimer:	I trust God.
Mathilda:	You say you trust Him, but how much?
Mortimer:	For everything! Like I said—He knows everything!
Mathilda:	Do you trust Him enough to thank Him for the bad things that happen to you?
Mortimer:	Oh! That's different!
Mathilda:	No, it isn't. Like you said, He knows everything, and He wants the best to happen to us, so sometimes what seems bad to *us* is really the best! God allows those things to happen to us so we'll *grow!*

Mortimer: I'm going to have to think about that a little while!

Mathilda: Well, okay. But when you can remember to thank God for everything in life, it means you *really* believe Him and you *really* trust Him!

Mortimer: Hmmm. What was that verse again?

Mathilda: "In every thing give thanks: for this is the will of God in Christ Jesus concerning you." First Thessalonians 5:18.

Mortimer: Hmmm. Are you sure it says EVERY THING?

Mathilda: Yes, I'm sure.

Mortimer: Well, okay. If God says it, I believe it. So *(pause)* I thank Him for all those bad things that happened to me this morning!

Mathilda: Hooray! You did it!

Mortimer: You know, it's not so hard to thank Him for the *good* things, but I'll have to keep reminding myself to thank Him for the bad ones.

Mathilda: Yeah, but when we can thank Him for the *bad* things, that really shows that we trust Him!

Mortimer: Say! Do you know what? I can think of a reason why God let those bad things happen to me this morning! If they hadn't, we wouldn't have talked about that verse! Then I wouldn't have known to thank Him for every thing!

Mathilda: It's a funny thing, but if we remember to thank Him for bad things, it's usually like that. He sends a thought to us that helps us see why it happened!

Mortimer: Yeah! That's a good verse, all right!

Mathilda: You ought to memorize it.

Mortimer: You're right. *(Turns to audience)* And I think all you guys out there should learn it, too!

Mathilda: Okay. Here it is again: "In every thing give thanks: for this is the will of God in Christ Jesus concerning you." First Thessalonians 5:18.

Mortimer: *(To audience)* Let's say it together! "In every thing give thanks: for this is the will of God in Christ Jesus concerning you." First Thessalonians 5:18.

Mathilda: That's pretty good. But you'd better try it again.

Mortimer: Okay, kids! Let's show Mathilda what a good job we can do! "In every thing give thanks: for this is the will of God in Christ Jesus concerning you." First Thessalonians 5:18.

Mathilda: *(To children)* I have to go now! But let's try not to forget that verse! Okay?

Mortimer: I have to go, too. *(To children)* See you all later!

(Mortimer and Mathilda leave stage together.)

Mortimer and Mathilda: Bye!

Script 10

WE CAN GIVE SOMETHING TO JESUS
(Christmas)

Inasmuch as ye have done it unto one of the least of these my brethren, you have done it unto me Matthew 25:40b.

(Mortimer and Mathilda are both on stage.)

Mortimer: Hi! What's the matter with you? It's almost Christmas! Children are supposed to be happy at Christmas!

Mathilda: Yeah, I know it. But I don't *feel* happy!

Mortimer: Why not? Is something wrong? Aren't you going to get any presents?

Mathilda: Sure. I'm going to get presents. I always do.

Mortimer: What are you so sad about then?

Mathilda: Well, I've been thinking.

Mortimer: Yeah?

Mathilda: Yeah. I'm getting old enough to *give* presents this year and. . . .

Mortimer: So, why don't you give some then?

Mathilda: Well, I've made presents for nearly everybody. And I've bought a few.

Mortimer: *(In a low voice)* Uh. Did you get one for, well, ah, for well, for. . . . Well, uh. . . .

Mathilda: *(Laughs)* Oh, silly. Of course, I got one for you!

Mortimer: Well, I sure don't see anything to be sad about then!

Mathilda: Mortimer, here's my problem. I have a present for people like you and my mom and my pop, but Christmas is *Jesus'* birthday, and I don't know how to give *Him* a present!

Mortimer: You're right. It *is* Jesus' birthday! Hmmm. We really should give Him something, shouldn't we?

Mathilda: See what I mean? How can I give *Jesus* a present?

Mortimer: Hmmm. There must be a way. Let me think. *(Pretends to think)* Hey! I know how!

Mathilda: You do? How?

Mortimer: Well, I remember a Bible verse about that!

Mathilda: A Bible verse? I don't remember any!

Mortimer: *(Thinking)* Let's see. I think it's found in Matthew 25:40. Yeah! That's where it is.

Mathilda: Well, tell me. What does it say?

Mortimer: It says, "Inasmuch as ye have done it unto the least of these my brethren, ye have done it unto me."

Mathilda: "Inasmuch as ye have done it unto the least of these my brethren, ye have done it unto me." How can that help me know how to give Jesus a Christmas present?

Mortimer: Well, we can't give Jesus anything *personally,* like a tie or some chocolates. But He says in Matthew 25:40 that you don't *have* to give anything to Him *personally!*

Mathilda: I don't know what you're talking about, Mortimer. What do you mean?

Mortimer: It means that when you give something to somebody who needs it, it's just like giving it to Jesus Himself.

Mathilda: Yeah. That makes sense, all right. But how can I find someone who needs something?

Mortimer: I bet you know lots of people that need things.

Mathilda: Hmmm. Let me think. . . .

Mortimer: How about your little sister? Your mom has to go to the store sometimes. You can help by taking care of Ellie when she goes.

Mathilda: Do you mean that would be doing something for Jesus?

Mortimer: Sure!

Mathilda: Wow! There are lots of things I can do for Jesus then! I can help my little brother with his arithmetic, too!

Mortimer: And you can help your mom do the dishes.

Mathilda: Yeah, and I can empty the trash. And, and. . . .

Mortimer: Now you've got the right idea.

Mathilda: And do you know what? I can give something to Jesus all year, not just at Christmas! I can help people all year long!

Mortimer: Yeah. You can even help *me* sometimes!

Mathilda: *(Laughs)* Yeah, I can even help you sometimes! *(Turns to audience)* That's a good verse Mortimer taught me. Why don't you say it with me? *(Repeat the verse slowly so the children can join in.)* "Inasmuch as ye have done it unto one of the least of these my brethren, ye have done it unto me" Matthew 25:40.

Mortimer: Say it with me, now. "Inasmuch as ye have done it unto one of the least of these my brethren, ye have done it unto me" Matthew 25:40.

Mathilda: *(Leaving)* I'm going home right now and start giving something to Jesus. Bye!

Mortimer: *(Follows Mathilda off stage)* Bye!

Script 11

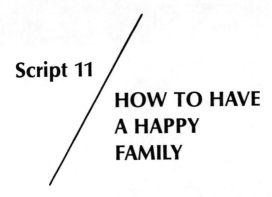

HOW TO HAVE A HAPPY FAMILY

Behold, how good and how pleasant it is for brethren to dwell together in unity Psalm 133:1.

(Mortimer is on the stage. Crying is heard off stage.)

Mortimer: Uh-oh. That sounds like Mathilda crying.

(Mathilda enters.)

Mortimer: Mathilda! What's the matter?

Mathilda: Oh, that sister of mine makes me so mad!

Mortimer: Why? Ellie's so nice and quiet. She wouldn't make anybody mad.

Mathilda: Oh, yeah? She makes *me* mad! She makes me *so* mad I could bite a nail in two!

Mortimer: That's pretty mad! It'd be hard on your teeth, though! What'd Ellie do?

Mathilda: Oh, she's a mess. She uses my pencils and doesn't sharpen them. She borrows my skates and then leaves them on the back porch. And just now she ate up all the candy that Aunt Hattie sent me.

Mortimer: Boy, she *is* a mess!

Mathilda: I wish I could make her quit doing things like that. But the more I yell at her and bawl her out, the worse she gets!

Mortimer:	*(Thinking)* Let's see. You yell at her and bawl her out.
Mathilda:	Uh-huh.
Mortimer:	*(Thinking)* And she gets worse.
Mathilda:	Uh-huh.
Mortimer:	Well, maybe you're going about it in the wrong way.
Mathilda:	Wrong way? What else can I do? I can't hit her! Mom won't let me!
Mortimer:	I know a Bible verse that says, "Behold, how good and how pleasant it is for brethren to dwell together in unity." It's found in Psalm 133:1.
Mathilda:	It says "brethren," and that means "brothers!"
Mortimer:	Oh, Mathilda, you know that means sisters, too!
Mathilda:	It *would* be nice to live together in peace, though, and I guess that's what unity means.
Mortimer:	It sure would. *(Pause)* I wonder how you could do it?
Mathilda:	I don't know. I've thought and thought about it. And the more I think, the madder I get!
Mortimer:	Well, it's pretty obvious getting mad doesn't help.
Mathilda:	Not a bit!
Mortimer:	Well, it's logical. You'll have to do something else!
Mathilda:	But what?
Mortimer:	Have you ever tried *not* getting mad?
Mathilda:	*Not* getting mad? You must be awful dumb. How can you *not* get mad when something just automatically makes you mad?
Mortimer:	Well, uh. I guess maybe you'd better ask God to help you if you can't do it yourself!

Mathilda: Well, I haven't tried that. Do you think it'd work?

Mortimer: It sure wouldn't hurt to try.

Mathilda: Okay. I'm going to pray right now. You pray with me. Dear God, I know I shouldn't get so mad at Ellie. And I know there'll never be any peace in our house as long as I keep on losing my temper. So, first, I'd like to ask You to forgive me. And then I'd like to ask You to help me not get so mad the next time Ellie messes up something that's mine. Amen.

Mortimer: That ought to help. If you really meant it. But don't forget, you've got to do your part, too. You've got to try not to get so mad next time. Just remember what·you prayed. Let Jesus help you.

Mathilda: I will. I really will. I just hate having all this fighting going on all the time at our house. And I just bet that if I stop getting mad myself things'll change for everybody!

Mortimer: Good for you, Mathilda! Maybe I'll come over and see you some time, if things sort of straighten up over there. Bye!

Mathilda: Bye, Mortimer. And thanks.

(Mortimer leaves off one side of stage. Mathilda goes off the other.)

Voice Behind the Curtain: The same time next week.

(Mortimer comes onto stage, talking to himself.)

Mortimer: I wonder how Mathilda and Ellie are getting along. Mathilda should know by now if not getting mad helps keep peace in her family. Here she comes now!

(Mathilda enters.)

Mathilda: Mortimer. Am I glad to see you!

Mortimer: You are? Why?

Mathilda: I've got so much to tell you! It worked! It really worked!

Mortimer: What worked?

Mathilda: My not letting myself get mad!

Mortimer: Hey! That's great!

Mathilda: You can say that again! Our house is so different you can hardly believe it!

Mortimer: Why? What happened?

Mathilda: Well, you and I prayed I wouldn't lose my temper last week. Remember?

Mortimer: Sure.

Mathilda: Well, it wasn't easy, but every time I felt like I was going to get mad, I just prayed and asked God to help me.

Mortimer: And did He?

Mathilda: He must have, because I'd stop and think before I said anything. And then I'd say something nice!

Mortimer: To whom?

Mathilda: To Ellie, mostly. She's the one who always bugged me the most. Anyway, when she got ink on my new dress, instead of getting mad I just told her I knew she didn't mean to and that it was all right. And do you know what she did?

Mortimer: No, what?

Mathilda: She started crying. She cried and cried. Until Mom came to see what was the matter. Mom thought I had hit her. But when Ellie told her what happened, Mom just kissed us both and said she'd see if she could get the ink out.

Mortimer: And could she?

Mathilda: She sure did.

Mortimer: Boy! That did work out a lot better than when you got mad about things.

Mathilda: And that's not the only time, either. And do you know what? Ellie's not bugging me nearly as much now. I don't know what's happened.

Mortimer: I don't either, but that verse in Psalms is really true, isn't it?

Mathilda: It sure is. I memorized it. "Behold, how good and pleasant it is for brethren to dwell together in unity" Psalm 133:1.

Mortimer: Yeah. I guess God really knows what He's talking about, doesn't He?

(Mathilda and Mortimer leave stage.)

Script 12

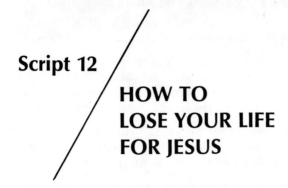

HOW TO LOSE YOUR LIFE FOR JESUS

He that findeth his life shall lose it; and he that loseth his life for my sake will find it Matthew 10:39.

(Enter Mortimer, sauntering along and whistling. When Mortimer reaches the middle of the stage, Mathilda rushes in.)

Mortimer: Hey! Wait a minute! Where are you going in such a hurry?

Mathilda: Oh, hi, Mortimer! I was just running an errand for Mrs. Thompson. She's that lady who lives next door to me, you know. She's sick.

Mortimer: Yeah. I heard she was sick.

Mathilda: I'm going to the store for her. She needs some eggs and potatoes.

Mortimer: You're awfully ambitious. How come you're going to the store for her? If you didn't, somebody else would.

Mathilda: You're probably right. But if *they* did, *I* couldn't!

Mortimer: You *couldn't?* Is something wrong with you? Do you *want* to do something you don't have to?

Mathilda: As a matter of fact, I do.

Mortimer: Boy! I sure wouldn't. I'm too busy doing my own things to bother with anybody else's.

Mathilda: Do you remember that Bible verse we learned last Sunday?

Mortimer: Oh, kinda. Let's see, it was about losing your life, wasn't it? Why? What does that have to do with your going to the store for Mrs. Thompson?

Mathilda: You remember the verse, "He that findeth his life shall lose it; and he that loseth his life for my sake shall find it." It's in Matthew 10:39.

Mortimer: "He who finds his life shall lose it, and he that loses his life for my sake shall find it." Yeah, that's Matthew 10:39, all right. But what does that have to do with your going to the store for Mrs. Thompson?

Mathilda: Oh, Mortimer, you must not have listened when our teacher explained what the verse means. You should pay attention when you go to church.

Mortimer: Oh, maybe. But sometimes I get tired. It's not easy for me to sit still very long, you know.

Mathilda: But if you *tried* to sit still, you could. And anyway, if you sat still, you'd learn a lot more.

Mortimer: Come on, Mathilda, tell me what "He who finds his life shall lose it, and he who loses his life for my sake shall find it" means.

Mathilda: Well, okay. In the first place, it's Jesus who's talking.

Mortimer: Jesus, huh? Well, it must be important, then. But I sure can't figure out what it means.

Mathilda: Well, I'll try to explain it to you, but you listen better next time our teacher explains something!

Mortimer: Okay. I'll try.

Mathilda: Well, Jesus is telling His disciples that He wants them to do things for Him.

Mortimer: *(Thoughtfully)* Yeah.

Mathilda: Jesus wanted His disciples to give their whole lives to Him. He said that if they would, they'd have a reward in heaven.

Mortimer: How could they give their whole lives to Him?

Mathilda: By doing things for Him. Like telling other people about Him, and doing good things because He said to do them.

Mortimer: But I don't have time to do stuff for *other* people all the time. I don't want to give *my* things up.

Mathilda: That's just what Jesus is saying. You really aren't giving anything worthwhile up. Because if you do just your own things they'll be forgotten. But if you do things for Jesus, He remembers them.

Mortimer: That doesn't sound like much fun to me!

Mathilda: No, I guess it doesn't. But the funny thing about it is that if you do what Jesus wants you to do, you're much happier right here on earth. And you don't miss out on a thing, because you stop *wanting* to do all that other stuff!

Mortimer: Well, I don't know.

Mathilda: Does Jesus want anything bad for you?

Mortimer: *(Slowly)* No.

Mathilda: Well, just believe what He says, and do it! Then you'll see how much fun it is!

Mortimer: Everything Jesus said is true, all right. So-o-o. Okay. I'll give it a chance!

Mathilda: Let's say that verse over again.

Mortimer: Okay.

Mathilda and Mortimer: "He who finds his life shall lose it, and he who loses his life for my sake shall find it" Matthew 10:39.

Mortimer: *(Looking at audience)* Hey, boys and girls, why don't you say it, too?

Mathilda and Mortimer: "He who finds his life shall lose it, and he who loses his life for my sake shall find it" Matthew 10:39.

Mortimer: *(To the audience)* Let's work on that verse, boys and girls. If Jesus said it, it must be right!

Mathilda: *(To the audience)* Yes, you better work on it. But in the meantime, I'd better hurry, so I can get Mrs. Thompson's eggs and potatoes.

(Mathilda hurries off stage. Mortimer starts after her.)

Mortimer: Hey, wait, Mathilda, I want to go with you. I want to start doing things for Jesus, too!

(Both exit.)

Script 13 / WHAT IS SIN?

For all have sinned, and come short of the glory of God
Romans 3:23.

(Mortimer and Mathilda enter.)

Mortimer: You know, I was just talking to Butch about becoming a Christian and I got stuck when I got to talking about sin. It's a new word to him.

Mathilda: Yes. I guess people who don't read the Bible or go to church don't understand some of the words we know. We get so used to hearing them we expect everybody to know what they mean.

Mortimer: I was trying to explain Romans 3:23 to Butch. You know, it says, "For all have sinned, and come short of the glory of God."

Mathilda: Yes. I know that verse. It's the one that made me realize that God couldn't even look at me until I accepted Jesus as my Savior.

Mortimer: It's a good verse. It makes people feel better when they understand *everybody* has sinned. Then they know they aren't different from anybody else.

Mathilda: Yes, and it helps us to know that there's no other way to get to God except through Jesus. We sure can't do it ourselves!

Mortimer: What would you say "sin" is, if somebody asked you?

Mathilda: Well, uh, let me see. Sin is evil. It's doing bad things.

Mortimer: Is that all?

Mathilda: Well, no. Not exactly.

Mortimer: What do you mean, not exactly?

Mathilda: Well, it's hard to explain, but sin is something we're born with!

Mortimer: How can a little baby do something wrong when it hasn't even been out of the hospital yet?

Mathilda: Well, it's because everyone is born in sin.

Mortimer: Everybody?

Mathilda: Well, except Adam and Eve.

Mortimer: Yeah, I know. They disobeyed God and did what the devil wanted them to do. They didn't think they had to depend on God. But they sure were sorry!

Mathilda: Yes, everybody else has been, too! Because when Adam and Eve sinned, they brought sin into the world and into everybody who would ever be born.

Mortimer: Sin is really not depending on or trusting God, isn't it? It's doing things our own way.

Mathilda: That's a good way to put it!

Mortimer: That's why we need to accept Jesus as our Savior. He's the only one who doesn't have sin in Him.

Mathilda: I'm glad God has made a way for our sins to be forgiven. If He hadn't sent Jesus, we'd never have been able to come into God's sight!

Mortimer: That's because God is so holy. He can't even look on sin!

Mathilda: And, just think, if we accept Jesus as our Savior, God doesn't see our sins at all, because Jesus took them all on the cross for us! That's what it means when people say He died for us.

Mortimer: Yeah. And all we have to do is accept Him as our Savior! That means we depend upon God, just like He wants us to!

Mathilda: God is really good, isn't He? He must love us an awful lot to send His Son to die so we wouldn't have to!

Mortimer: Romans 3:23 says, "For all have sinned, and come short of the glory of God." But I'm glad God put John 3:16 in the Bible, too, so we'd know how to get to God.

Mathilda: Yeah. "For God so loved the world, that he gave his only begotten Son, that whosoever believeth in him should not perish, but have everlasting life."

Mortimer: We couldn't ever repay God for what He's done for us.

Mathilda: No. It all depends on Jesus. And what we do with Him!

Mortimer: Let's go over Romans 3:23 again.

Mathilda: Okay. "For all have sinned and come short of the glory of God" Romans 3:23.

Mortimer: Hey! I have a question!

Mathilda: What is it?

Mortimer: It's about little babies. We said everybody is born in sin. And little babies are too little to accept Jesus. They can't even talk!

Mathilda: You're right, Mortimer. They can't!

Mortimer: What happens to them if they die before they accept Jesus?

Mathilda: Well, I'm sure God can take care of that. I'm glad He knows everything and that He loves us so much.

Mortimer: That's it! God understands everything a lot better than we do.

Mathilda: And He's not going to do anything bad. So He takes care of all that for little babies until they're big enough to let Jesus come into their hearts.

Mortimer: I'm glad God loves us so much. Aren't you?

Mathilda: Yes, but when we're big enough to understand about Jesus and how He died for our sins, He expects us to let Jesus come into our hearts.

Mortimer: I'm glad He put it all in the Bible for us! *(Thoughtfully)* "For all have sinned, and come short of the glory of God" Romans 3:23.

Mathilda: *(Turning to audience)* Hey, kids! You say it with us this time. Okay?

Mortimer and Mathilda: "For all have sinned, and come short of the glory of God" Romans 3:23.

Mortimer: That's a good verse to remember, kids! Don't forget it!

Mathilda: No. Don't forget it, because every time you say it you can remember how much God loves you!

Mortimer: Well, we've gotta go now. Bye!

Mathilda: Bye!

(Mortimer and Mathilda leave stage.)

Script 14

GOD HATES LYING

These six things doth the Lord hate: yea, seven are an abomination unto him: A proud look, a lying tongue, and hands that shed innocent blood, An heart that deviseth wicked imaginations, feet that be swift in running to mischief, A false witness that speaketh lies, and he that soweth discord among brethren Proverbs 6:16-19.

(Mortimer enters stage.)

Mortimer: *(Walking back and forth)* Oh, dear. Oh, dear. Am I in a mess! Oh, dear!

(Mathilda enters.)

Mathilda: Hi, Mortimer!

Mortimer: Hi.

Mathilda: You don't look so good! What's the matter?

Mortimer: Oh, nothing.

Mathilda: Well, you sure *look* like something's wrong!

Mortimer: Boy! I've just realized I've got into a terrible habit!

Mathilda: I *thought* something was wrong!

Mortimer: I even did it to you just then!

Mathilda: You did? What did you do to me?

Mortimer: I lied to you!

Mathilda:	You did? I didn't know.
Mortimer:	That's the trouble. Lots of times the person you lie to doesn't know, so you think you're getting away with it. But you're not. God knows.
Mathilda:	That's right. God knows everything. But what did you lie to me about?
Mortimer:	I just told you nothing was wrong with me . . . and something *was.*
Mathilda:	Oh.
Mortimer:	It has become as easy for me to tell a lie as it is to tell the truth.
Mathilda:	Boy! You *do* have a bad habit!
Mortimer:	Yeah. And bad habits are a lot easier to *make* than to *break!*
Mathilda:	And lying is an easy bad habit to get into, isn't it?
Mortimer:	It sure is. And once you tell a lie, it grows.
Mathilda:	Yeah. You have to tell another lie to cover up the first one.
Mortimer:	And another, and another!
Mathilda:	And God doesn't want us to lie!
Mortimer:	I know it. I was just reading some verses in the Book of Proverbs in the Bible. And they said that God *hates* lying!
Mathilda:	I always thought God was a God of love!
Mortimer:	He is! But He hates evil things.
Mathilda:	Then, I guess He does hate lying.
Mortimer:	Yeah. It's funny, but in these verses it says God hates lying twice. In two things out of seven, it says God hates lying!
Mathilda:	I don't remember those verses. What are they?

Mortimer: They're found in Proverbs 6:16 through 19. "These six things doth the Lord hate: yea, seven are an abomination unto him: A proud look, a lying tongue, and hands that shed innocent blood, An heart that deviseth wicked imaginations, feet that be swift in running to mischief, A false witness that speaketh lies, and he that soweth discord among brethren."

Mathilda: Say, it does mention lying twice! That must mean God really, *really* hates lying!

Mortimer: That's what I've been trying to tell you!

Mathilda: I guess you *do* have a problem!

Mortimer: Can you help me, Mathilda? Can you help me stop lying?

Mathilda: Boy! I don't think so. Only God could do that. But you've got to *let* Him!

Mortimer: How?

Mathilda: Well, you've made a good start. You know you're sinning when you lie.

Mortimer: If that's a good start, I have a good start, all right! Wow! Do I have a good start!

Mathilda: I think the next thing you should do is to ask God to forgive you for all the lies you've told.

Mortimer: Okay. What next?

Mathilda: Ask Him to help you *not* tell them any more. Ask Him to remind you when you're doing it so you can stop before you tell it. Or at least before you finish it!

Mortimer: Okay! But it won't be easy!

Mathilda: And then, everytime you forget and tell a lie, ask God right then to forgive you.

Mortimer: Out loud?

Mathilda:	Well, I don't think that's necessary. But you'll want to change your lie to the truth right then. And you'll have to do *that* out loud!
Mortimer:	You mean I have to tell the person I lied to that I lied to them?
Mathilda:	I guess so. After all, if you're really sorry, you don't want to leave them thinking the lie is the truth, do you?
Mortimer:	Well, no.
Mathilda:	If you do those things, I bet you'll stop lying in no time!
Mortimer:	Thanks, Mathilda. I'm going to start right now! Oh, say, I've got a question. What if somebody asks me something I don't want to tell them. Is it all right to lie then?
Mathilda:	No, of course not! Just tell them the truth! Tell them you don't *want* to tell them!
Mortimer:	Yeah! I guess I *could* do that! Well, I'm going now! I'll be seeing you!
Mathilda:	Bye!

(Mortimer leaves stage. Mathilda follows.)

Voice Off Stage: The next day.

(Mortimer comes onto stage.)

Mortimer:	Boy! I can hardly wait until I see Mathilda! I've got some great news to tell her!

(Mathilda enters.)

Mathilda:	Hi, Mortimer! You sure look a lot better today than you did yesterday!
Mortimer:	I feel lots better, too! I've been doing what you told me to do about lying, and God has really been helping me!

Mathilda: Great!

Mortimer: It hasn't been easy, but every time I start to tell a lie, I stop and think and then I tell the truth . . . or, like you said, I just tell 'em I don't want to tell 'em and *that's* the truth!

Mathilda: You look a lot more rested today, too.

Mortimer: Yeah. I should. And do you know why?

Mathilda: No, why?

Mortimer: Well, last night when my Mom asked me to turn my light off and go to bed, I did.

Mathilda: Don't you always?

Mortimer: Well, I always go to bed. But I've been turning on the flashlight under the covers and reading.

Mathilda: Oh! So that's why you looked so tired lately!

Mortimer: Uh-huh. When Mom called in before, I told her my light was off, but I knew I was lying.

Mathilda: Your *flashlight* was on, wasn't it?

Mortimer: Yeah. Anyway, last night when she asked me, I told her I'd turn it off, and I did. And I didn't turn my flashlight on, either. Then there wasn't anything to do but go to sleep!

Mathilda: Which is what you needed to do all the time!

Mortimer: Uh-huh.

Mathilda: What were you going to tell me?

Mortimer: Oh. All that. But most important, I wanted to tell you how *great* I feel!

Mathilda: I know what you mean! I always feel good, too, when I do what I know God wants me to do!

Mortimer: I know how to be a Christian. To take Jesus into my heart. But now I know how to be a *happy* Christian! It's to obey God! Hee hee! *(Dances around)*

Mathilda: Yeah. We miss out on all of God's blessings when we don't trust and obey Him.

Mortimer: That's the name of a song, isn't it?

Mathilda: Yeah! It is! I never thought of that!

Mortimer: How does it go now?

Mathilda: Something like this, I think. *(Sings)* Trust and obey, for there's no other way to be happy in Jesus, but to trust and obey.

(Mortimer and Mathilda leave stage.)

Script 15

WHAT
IS A
TITHE?

Bring ye all the tithes into the storehouse, that there may be meat in mine house, and prove me now herewith, saith the Lord of hosts, if I will not open you the windows of heaven, and pour you out a blessing, that there shall not be room enough to receive it Malachi 3:10.

(Mortimer and Mathilda enter stage together.)

Mathilda: Did you remember to bring your offering to church today?

Mortimer: Well, yeah. In a way. I had a dime in this coat pocket left over from my shopping trip downtown last week. I'll just put that in. How much've you got?

Mathilda: Thirty cents.

Mortimer: Thirty cents! Wow! That's a lot of money! How come you're going to put all that in the offering?

Mathilda: Well, I believe in giving more than my tithe. My tithe is twenty-five cents. And I'm going to give the other nickel just because I love Jesus so much!

Mortimer: Uh. Wait a minute. I understand that stuff about giving a love gift because you love Jesus, but what's that other stuff mean?

Mathilda: Oh, you mean, tithing?

Mortimer: Yeah. Tithing. What's that?

Mathilda: Well, a tithe is what the people in the Old Testament were supposed to give God.

Mortimer: You mean money? How much?

Mathilda: Well, you have to be kind of smart to know what a tithe is. You have to know a little arithmetic.

Mortimer: Okay. I know a little arithmetic.

Mathilda: Do you know what a percentage is?

Mortimer: Well, sort of. It's a part of something. Like if you have one hundred percent of something, you have ALL of it!

Mathilda: Right! If you have ALL of something, you have one hundred percent of it.

Mortimer: Okay. So what does that have to do with a tithe?

Mathilda: Well, a title is ten percent of something.

Mortimer: Oh!

Mathilda: Like a tithe of a dollar is ten cents!

Mortimer: I see. It takes one hundred pennies to make a dollar. So ten pennies is one-tenth of a dollar. Is that right?

Mathilda: Yeah! You surprise me! I didn't think you could do it. And a tenth of ten pennies is one penny. Now, how much is a tithe of ten dollars?

Mortimer: Uh. A tithe of ten dollars. That would be one-tenth of ten dollars. If one-tenth of ten pennies is one penny, then. . . . One dollar!

Mathilda: That's right!

Mortimer: Explain it to me once more, Mathilda. I don't know if I can remember all that.

Mathilda: Well, I'll try. But it's hard to explain.

Mortimer: See! That's why it's so hard to understand!

Mathilda: Well, I'll try. Listen closely.

Mortimer: *(Moves up closer to Mathilda)* Is this close enough?

Mathilda: Oh, silly. I mean *listen* closer, not get closer to me!

Mortimer: Okay. Okay. Go ahead. I'm listening.

Mathilda: Okay. One hundred percent of anything is all of it.

Mortimer: One hundred percent of anything is all of it. Okay. I've got that.

Mathilda: So. Take a dollar. How many pennies are there in a dollar?

Mortimer: One hundred.

Mathilda: Okay. If you had a hundred pennies you'd have a dollar. Right?

Mortimer: Right!

Mathilda: Ten percent of a hundred pennies would be how much?

Mortimer: *(Uncertainly)* Ten pennies?

Mathilda: Right. The people of the Old Testament were supposed to give a tithe of everything they had to God. But, of course, they didn't have money in those days. They had things like corn and wheat and cattle. But it means the same things. They were supposed to give ten parts of all they had.

Mortimer: I think it's a lot easier to tithe with money, though. You wouldn't have to measure all that corn and wheat out.

Mathilda: That sounds just like you! Anyway, that's what a tithe is.

Mortimer: So that's what a tithe is. But, Mathilda, isn't that from the Old Testament? Are we supposed to give a tithe, too? We don't live under the law like the people back then. Do we have to give a tithe now?

Mathilda: No, we don't *have* to do anything. But I think we should give at *least* as much as the Old Testament people, don't you?

Mortimer: Yeah. Because we know all about Jesus and what He's done for us.

Mathilda: That's why I'm giving the extra nickel.

Mortimer: And the quarter is your tithe?

Mathilda: Yes. I earned $2.50 this week, and one-tenth of $2.50 is twenty-five cents.

Mortimer: *(Thoughtfully)* Uh. Oh. You made $2.50. That's a new problem, isn't it? How do you figure that?

Mathilda: Well, ten pennies is a tithe of one hundred pennies. Right?

Mortimer: Right.

Mathilda: So five pennies is a tithe of fifty pennies.

Mortimer: *(Mumbling)* Five pennies is a tithe of fifty cents.

Mathilda: So, from my two dollars and fifty cents, I tithe ten cents out of the first dollar and ten cents out of the second dollar and five cents out of my fifty cents.

Mortimer: Oh, dear. I think I should tithe, all right. You convinced me of that. But I think I'll just earn a dollar a week. Then my tithe will be ten cents. That won't be so hard to figure!

(Both start walking off stage.)

Mathilda: Silly! It's not hard! Just listen. Ten pennies is one tenth of a dollar. . . . *(Voice gets lower and lower as they leave the stage.)*

Script 16

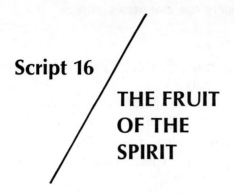

THE FRUIT OF THE SPIRIT

But the fruit of the Spirit is love, joy, peace, longsuffering, gentleness, goodness, faith, meekness, temperance: against such there is no law Galatians 5:22, 23.

(Mortimer and Mathilda enter.)

Mortimer: La de da. I feel so good today! I feel just great!

Mathilda: I do, too! La de da! La de da!

Mortimer: I feel like I just love everybody!

Mathilda: I do, too!

Mortimer: What do you suppose has got into us?

Mathilda: I don't know, but it's great to feel this way, isn't it?

Mortimer: It sure is. I feel so close to God!

Mathilda: Yeah!

Mortimer: I feel like I have all the patience in the world.

Mathilda: Yeah! I feel like really being a good big sister!

Mortimer: *(Laughs)* I guess I can't do that!

Mathilda: No, but you could be patient and gentle and kind with Ernie, that little boy who lives next door to you!

Mortimer: Yeah! I even feel like that!

Mathilda: I feel like God can depend on me!

Mortimer: And people, too!

Mathilda: But I don't feel proud about all these things, just humble and grateful.

Mortimer: And I feel like I can really do what God wants me to . . . with His help, of course!

Mathilda: Oh, yes, all of this has to be with His help!

Mortimer: You're right! Say! I just thought of something!

Mathilda: What?

Mortimer: Do you know what we just named?

Mathilda: We've named something?

Mortimer: Yeah! The fruit of the Spirit!

Mathilda: We did? What's that?

Mortimer: Well, that's what's in a Christian who loves God and has confessed all his sins and is filled with the Holy Spirit!

Mathilda: It is? Wow! That's sort of the way I am right now, too!

Mortimer: There are two verses in Galatians 5, verses 22 and 23! They say, "But the fruit of the Spirit is love, joy, peace, longsuffering, gentleness, goodness, faith, meekness, temperance: against such there is no law."

Mathilda: I guess there wouldn't be any law against those things! They're all so good!

Mortimer: Did you recognize them when I named them?

Mathilda: Well, you went pretty fast. Say them again.

Mortimer: Well, the first one is love.

Mathilda: That's God's love, isn't it? Isn't God's love different from our regular kind of love?

Mortimer: It sure is! It's different because you don't have to *feel* God's love. God's love is a matter of *deciding* to love someone more than *feeling* love for them! Then God can love through you!

Mathilda: Okay. What's the second one?

Mortimer: Joy.

Mathilda: I like that one. I'm glad God wants us to have joy and happiness and that He gives it to us.

Mortimer: The next one is "peace."

Mathilda: If you're right with God, you do have peace, don't you? Things don't bother you because you know God takes care of everything, and you just let Him do it!

Mortimer: Yeah. And the next one is "longsuffering."

Mathilda: *(Laughs)* That *has* to come from God for sure! Longsuffering is being even more patient than patient!

Mortimer: That's a good way to put it. It means to forgive people and forgive them and forgive them and to keep on forgiving them! That's what God does for us!

Mathilda: Love, joy, peace, longsuffering. That's four. How many fruits of the Spirit are there?

Mortimer: Nine all together. The next is "gentleness."

Mathilda: That's a good one, too. We should be gentle and easy with people, taking care not to hurt their feelings.

Mortimer: Right! And the next one is "goodness."

Mathilda: I think goodness must be doing what God wants us to do.

Mortimer: I think so, too. Because if we do what He wants us to do, we'll be good, all right. We sure won't be bad!

Mathilda: Love, joy, peace, longsuffering, gentleness, goodness. That's six. That leaves three more!

Mortimer: Yeah! The next one is "faith." I think that really means faithfulness. You know, like keeping your word and doing what you say you'll do.

Mathilda: Oh. Let's see. Love, joy, peace, longsuffering, gentleness, goodness, faith. That leaves two more.

Mortimer: "Meekness" is the next one.

Mathilda: What does it mean to be meek?

Mortimer: It means to be humble and doing what Jesus would do. Not being pushy.

Mathilda: Oh! Let's see, now. Love, joy, peace, longsuffering, gentleness, goodness, faith, and meekness. That leaves one more!

Mortimer: And that's "temperance." That's self-discipline!

Mathilda: Self-discipline! That's a good one, too! It really takes that to stay close to God. If you don't have self-discipline and decide to do something and do it, you don't ever get anything done! To keep close to God, you have to just keep asking God to forgive you and to fill you with His Spirit.

Mortimer: I never thought of it that way before. But you're right! Every time you slip, you kinda have to start all over again!

Mathilda: Let's say the verses again. Okay. "But the fruit of the Spirit is love, joy, peace, longsuffering, gentleness, goodness, faith, meekness, temperance: against such there is no law" Galatians 5:22, 23. Say! That's pretty good! Let's go over the fruit again.

Mortimer: Okay. Love.

Mathilda: Joy.

Mortimer: Peace.

Mathilda: Longsuffering.

Mortimer: Gentleness.

Mathilda: Goodness.

Mortimer: Faith.

Mathilda: Meekness.

Mortimer: And temperance!

Mathilda: Against such there is no law!

Mortimer: *(Turns to audience)* See if you can say them now! Okay? Say it with me: "But the fruit of the Spirit is love, joy, peace, longsuffering, gentleness, goodness, faith, meekness, temperance: against such there is no law."

Mathilda: I'm glad you knew that verse, Mortimer. It's really great to know that God wants us to have all those things. Well, I have to go now. Bye!

Mortimer: Bye!

(Mathilda and Mortimer leave stage.)

Script 17

MEEK ISN'T SISSY!

Blessed are the meek; for they shall inherit the earth Matthew 5:5.

(Mortimer and Mathilda enter stage.)

Mathilda: I just saw that new kid Butch down the street. He's the worst bully I ever saw!

Mortimer: Yeah, I've heard he's pretty mean. I think he could be a nice guy if he'd stop picking on other kids.

Mathilda: Yeah. And he always picks on kids littler than he is, too!

Mortimer: Sure. He'd be dumb to pick on somebody bigger!

Mathilda: Oh, you know what I mean! Does he ever pick on you?

Mortimer: No. I'm almost as big as he is. And I guess I've never been around when he picked on anybody else, either.

Mathilda: If he did pick on you, what would you do?

Mortimer: Oh, I don't know.

Mathilda: If he picked on littler kids when you were around, what would you do?

Mortimer: I guess I never thought about it much.

Mathilda: Hmmm. I wonder what Jesus would do.

Mortimer: I don't know, but one of the things he said to His disciples was "Blessed are the meek; for they shall inherit the earth." That's in Matthew 5:5.

Mathilda: I've always wondered what meek was. It sounds sort of sissy to me!

Mortimer: Well, Jesus sure wasn't any sissy. And *He* was meek!

Mathilda: Yeah, that's right!

Mortimer: He wasn't scared of anything!

Mathilda: Nope! But He sure didn't pick any fights, either!

Mortimer: And something else, when people picked on Him, He didn't try to defend Himself, either!

Mathilda: That's right! He didn't have to die like He died. He could have just said the word and all those mean men who killed Him would have dropped dead!

Mortimer: That sure isn't being a sissy!

Mathilda: I bet He'd have stepped in and helped someone who was being hurt, though.

Mortimer: Sure He would have! Hey! That's my answer! If I ever see Butch picking on somebody, I'll have to step in and stop him. I don't like to fight. But neither did Jesus!

Mathilda: I guess what we have to remember is to be like Him, isn't it?

Mortimer: Yeah. We should always stop and think, "What would Jesus do?" and then DO IT!

Mathilda: Well, I'll see you later.

Mortimer: Yeah, I've got to go, too.

(Mortimer and Mathilda leave the stage.)

Voice Behind Stage: The next day.

(Mortimer and Mathilda enter stage.)

Mathilda: Hey! You look like you've been in a fight!

Mortimer: *(Groan.)* Have I been in a fight!?! *(Groan.)*

Mathilda: What happened?

Mortimer: Well, it's a funny thing. But we were talking about that verse Matthew 5:5 yesterday. . . .

Mathilda: Oh, you mean, "Blessed are the meek, for they shall inherit the earth?"

Mortimer: Yeah. Well, it's a good thing we talked about it.

Mathilda: Why?

Mortimer: Well, I met Butch right after that.

Mathilda: Uh-oh.

Mortimer: Yeah, uh-oh. *(Groan.)*

Mathilda: Did he beat you up?

Mortimer: He sure did.

Mathilda: What did you do?

Mortimer: Well, I tried to do what I thought Jesus would do.

Mathilda: What was that?

Mortimer: Well, I remembered Jesus didn't defend Himself.

Mathilda: Oh, no! You mean you let Butch hit you and you didn't hit him back?

Mortimer: That's what I did! *(Groan.)*

Mathilda: Oh, Mortimer. How brave you are!

Mortimer: You know, you're right! It takes more courage NOT to fight back than it does to fight!

Mathilda: What did Butch think about that?

Mortimer: *(Laughs)* He didn't know what to think! He called me a sissy!

Mathilda: What did you tell him?

Mortimer: I just told him he could think I was a sissy if he wanted to, but I wanted to be meek like Jesus.

Mathilda: He must have thought you were crazy!

Mortimer: Yeah. That's what he said!

Mathilda: Oh, Mortimer. That was so brave of you. I bet you could beat him up easy if you wanted to.

Mortimer: Yeah, I can.

Mathilda: You sound so certain. Do you really think you can?

Mortimer: I *know* I can. Because I *did!*

Mathilda: You *did?* I thought you just said. . . .

Mortimer: I'm not finished telling you what happened yet!

Mathilda: What else happened?

Mortimer: Well, he saw it wasn't any fun fighting me since I wouldn't fight back, so he left me. Then he saw some littler kids down the street and went after them.

Mathilda: Uh-oh!

Mortimer: Then I followed him and told him to quit, but he wouldn't.

Mathilda: Oh, that was terrible.

Mortimer: Well, not really. Because I just tapped him on the shoulder and told him to stop hitting those little kids and. . . .

Mathilda: And. . . .

Mortimer: And he called me a sissy and turned around and started hitting them again, and then. . . .

Mathilda: And then?

Mortimer: I just told him to pick on somebody his own size and belted him one!

Mathilda: Oh, Mortimer!

Mortimer: And do you know what?

Mathilda: No, what?

Mortimer: He was so surprised, he just stood there.

Mathilda: I bet he was surprised, after you wouldn't fight him before!

Mortimer: He looked so surprised, I just started laughing. Then the little kids got to laughing. And the first thing we knew, Butch was laughing, too!

Mathilda: *(Laughs)* I bet that was funny! Then what happened?

Mortimer: Well, when we finally stopped laughing, Butch looked at me and said, "Hey, you've got quite a right there! And I thought you were a sissy!"

Mathilda: I knew you weren't any sissy, Mortimer!

Mortimer: Yeah, and I told him about being meek because Jesus was meek and being meek didn't mean you were a sissy. And do you know what?

Mathilda: No, what?

Mortimer: He and I are friends now! And he's going to go to church with me! He said he wanted to know more about Jesus!

Mathilda: Oh, Mortimer, that's wonderful. You know that must be what the rest of that verse means. You know, about inheriting the earth.

Mortimer: Yeah! We can't get things by force. And we'll be rewarded when we stay out of fights. That's a good verse.

Mathilda: Matthew 5:5. "Blessed are the meek, for they shall inherit the earth." It's easy to learn, too!

(Mortimer and Mathilda leave stage.)

Script 18

PARENTS REALLY DO KNOW SOMETHING!

Children, obey your parents in the Lord: for this is right
Ephesians 6:1.

(Mortimer and Mathilda enter.)

Mathilda: I don't know why we have that same verse in children's church so much.

Mortimer: Yeah. I don't either.

Mathilda: Maybe it's because grownups think we need it a lot!

Mortimer: No wonder. After all, it's to their benefit!

Mathilda: *(Thoughtfully)* "Children, obey your parents in the Lord: for this is right" Ephesians 6:1.

Mortimer: I guess I only knew the first part of that verse before. There's more to it than just, "Children, obey your parents."

Mathilda: Yeah. I'm glad Miss Brown explained the rest of the verse this time.

Mortimer: Yeah. I guess different people have different ideas about what the Bible says. What do you think that part about "In the Lord" means?

Mathilda: I don't know. But I can sure see why you can take it two different ways.

Mortimer: Yeah. Like it *could* mean that you only have to obey your parents if they love Jesus. It kinda sounds that way.

Mathilda: Yes, but I don't think that's what it means. I think that *children* who love Jesus should obey their parents.

Mortimer: Like the verses on obeying the government. They say you should obey the law, but I think there's one time you shouldn't.

Mathilda: Really? Like when?

Mortimer: Like if the government made you do something to disobey God.

Mathilda: Oh! I see! Because God has more authority than the government!

Mortimer: What does that mean?

Mathilda: Well, we should *always* obey God. The Bible tells us that over and over again.

Mortimer: Yeah.

Mathilda: So, we obey God *in all things.* We shouldn't ever do anything God says we're not supposed to do—even if the government tells us to.

Mortimer: Or if our parents tell us to?

Mathilda: Yes.

Mortimer: Well, that sounds to me like either way you say it, it means the same thing, then.

Mathilda: *(Thoughtfully)* Let's see. Children in the Lord, obey your parents. Yeah. I see what you mean!

Mortimer: See, if we're in the Lord, we're supposed to obey our parents.

Mathilda: Yeah! And then, "Children, obey your parents in the Lord" means that we're supposed to obey our parents in everything, *except* if they tell us to disobey God!

Mortimer: I don't think that's so hard to understand!

Mathilda: "Children, obey your parents in the Lord: for this is right," Ephesians 6:1.

Mortimer: Have your folks ever made you do something that made you disobey God?

Mathilda: No, come to think of it. I can't remember that they have!

Mortimer: Mine either! But I know a kid who'd have trouble if he knew this verse.

Mathilda: Really? That'd be terrible to have that problem.

Mortimer: This kid's dad wants him to *steal!*

Mathilda: No kidding? Does he do it?

Mortimer: Yeah. His dad even showed him how!

Mathilda: That's awful! Boy! What would *you* do if your dad told you to do that?

Mortimer: I don't know. If he got real mean about it, it would be hard not to do it!

Mathilda: Yeah.

Mortimer: I know one thing I'd do. I'd ask God to help me.

Mathilda: Yeah. You'd sure need *His* help, all right!

Mortimer: Then, I'd . . . I'd. . . .

Mathilda: Well, for one thing, you'd have to be careful how you talked to your dad!

Mortimer: Yeah. If you got fresh, he'd probably smack you or something.

Mathilda: But if you used that chance to be nice and told him why you couldn't do it, you might even get to tell him about Jesus!

Mortimer: Wouldn't it be fantastic if you could do that?

Mathilda: Yeah. But it'd sure be hard.

Mortimer: God would help you though, if you let Him.

Mathilda: I know He would. You'd just have to be careful not to do it in your *own* way, but in *His!*

Mortimer: I guess we're pretty lucky, having our parents.

Mathilda: Yeah. I never thought about parents making kids do *bad* things before.

Mortimer: You know, I complain a lot about all the stuff my parents make me do, but, come to think of it, wouldn't it be terrible if kids didn't have somebody to take care of them?

Mathilda: Wow! Just think! All those little babies with nobody to feed them or cover them up when it's cold!

Mortimer: Yeah, and all the school kids who wouldn't have anybody to fix their lunches and wash their clothes!

Mathilda: And all the college kids who wouldn't have somebody to help them through college!

Mortimer: And all the married kids who wouldn't have a babysitter!

Mathilda: *(Laughs)* We're really getting carried away, aren't we?

Mortimer: Yes, but it's true.

Mathilda: And it's *right!*

Mortimer: That's right! The verse says so! "Children, obey your parents in the Lord: for this is right," Ephesians 6:1.

Mathilda: How about teaching it to all those kids out there, Mortimer?

Mortimer: Okay. Let's all say it together! Ready, kids? Okay! Go! "Children, obey your parents in the Lord: for this is right," Ephesians 6:1.

Mathilda: Let's do it again! "Children, obey your parents in the Lord: for this is right," Ephesians 6:1.

Mortimer: We have to go now, but remember, kids, God says it's right to obey our parents!

Mathilda: Bye!

Mortimer: Bye!

(Mortimer and Mathilda wave and leave the stage.)

Script 19

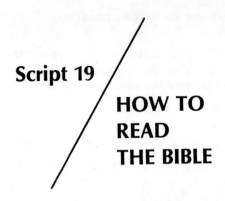

HOW TO READ THE BIBLE

All scripture is given by inspiration of God, and is profitable for doctrine, for reproof, for correction, for instruction in righteousness: that the man of God may be perfect, thoroughly furnished unto all good works II Timothy 3:16.

(Mortimer and Mathilda are on the stage.)

Mathilda: I sure am glad we have the Bible, aren't you, Mortimer?

Mortimer: Yeah. Because we'd hardly be able to know anything God wants us to know, if we didn't.

Mathilda: I have to admit, though. I really don't always get a lot out of it when I read it. Do you?

Mortimer: Well, I hate to say it, but no, I don't either. *(Looks around)* You won't tell anyone I said that, will you?

Mathilda: No, not if you don't want me to. But I think that's what our trouble is!

Mortimer: What?

Mathilda: We're too proud to admit we don't understand it! People keep telling us to read it, so they must think we know how, but since nobody tells them we don't, they can't help us!

Mortimer: Maybe you're right. But do you suppose they *could* help us? After all, how can anybody help *us* understand something when *we* read it?

Mathilda: It does seem like it's pretty much up to us at that!

Mortimer: But maybe we could help each other?

Mathilda: If grownups can't help us, how can we help each other?

Mortimer: I don't know. But we can try!

Mathilda: Okay. Start thinking of a way. And I will, too.

(They are quiet a short time.)

Mortimer: Hey! I thought of something!

Mathilda: What?

Mortimer: Well, in the first place, some Bibles are harder to read than others. Lots of people have written different versions of the Bible, but they are really the same Bible. They all say the same thing, but in a different way.

Mathilda: Yeah, but how does that help us?

Mortimer: Well, we should find a Bible *we* can understand!

Mathilda: That makes sense. Some people say it's easier to memorize verses from the King James version, but sometimes I don't understand what it's saying when I read it!

Mortimer: I don't either. But then different people like different versions, or there wouldn't be so many!

Mathilda: That's right. I might like one, and you might like another. But the important thing is to use the one you like best!

Mortimer: Okay, so that's rule number one. Use a version of the Bible that I can understand the best.

Mathilda: I have another rule!

Mortimer:	What?
Mathilda:	Well, since the Bible is God talking to us, it seems to me that it would make sense if we asked Him to help us understand what He's trying to tell us!
Mortimer:	You mean we should pray before we read it? Hey! That's good!
Mathilda:	Okay. So rule number one is: Use a version of the Bible that I can understand the best. Rule number two is: Ask God to help me understand it.
Mortimer:	That's great! You know I bet just those two rules will help us! Can you think of any more?
Mathilda:	Well, we have to help God. So how about saying something like "try to figure out what God is saying to me?"
Mortimer:	I don't know why we can't use that. After all, we can't expect God to do everything!
Mathilda:	Okay. Rule number one is: Use a version of the Bible that I can understand the best.
Mortimer:	Rule number two is: Ask God to help me understand it.
Mathilda:	And rule number three is: Try to figure out what God is saying to me.
Mortimer:	I know another one! Believe it!
Mathilda:	What do you mean, "believe it"?
Mortimer:	Well, when we read the Bible, we shouldn't try to excuse ourselves and say we can't do this or that. We should just take God at His Word!
Mathilda:	You're right! Sometimes I do understand what God is saying, but I pretend not to, or say that it isn't for me, or something like that. I should do what you said. I should believe it!
Mortimer:	Okay. Rule number four is: Believe it!

Mathilda: Hey, these are really some good ideas! Rule number one is: Use a version of the Bible that I can understand the best. Rule number two is: Ask God to help me understand it. Rule number three is: Try to figure out what God is saying to me. And. . . .

Mortimer: And rule number four is: Believe it!

Mathilda: And I can think of one more. It really isn't about reading the Bible, but it goes along with it.

Mortimer: Yeah? What?

Mathilda: Well, if we read the Bible and understand it and believe it, we should DO what it says!

Mortimer: That's great! Sure! That gives us five rules. If we can do all of those, we won't be wasting our time when we read the Bible. Hey, I'm getting all excited!

Mathilda: Me, too! I'm going home right now to read my Bible!

Mortimer: Yeah. Me, too. I know I'll understand it better. And I want to write those rules down before I forget them! Let's say them once more. Okay?

Mortimer and Mathilda together:

Rule 1: Use a version of the Bible I can understand.

Rule 2: Ask God to help me understand it.

Rule 3: Try to figure out what God is saying to me.

Rule 4: Believe it.

Rule 5: DO it!

(Mortimer and Mathilda hurry off stage.)

Script 20

LIFE CAN BE EXCITING!

If ye know these things, happy are ye if ye do them John 13:17.

(Mathilda enters stage singing happily. Mortimer follows her. He is walking slowly.)

Mortimer: Ho hum.

Mathilda: "Ho hum"? What's the matter with you?

Mortimer: Oh, I'm just bored.

Mathilda: Bored? I've heard of old people getting bored! But you're just a kid!

Mortimer: Maybe I'm just a kid, but all the same, I'm bored!

Mathilda: Boy! That's too bad!

Mortimer: Why? Don't you ever get bored?

Mathilda: Not very often. Life is too wonderful and exciting to be bored!

Mortimer: Wonderful and exciting? What's so wonderful and exciting about getting up at the same time every morning, eating breakfast, going to school, going home and eating supper and watching TV and going to bed every day?

Mathilda: The way you look at it, no wonder you're bored!

Mortimer: The way I look at what? TV?

Mathilda: No, silly. At life.

Mortimer: What's to look at? That's just the way it is!

Mathilda: Oh, but there's so much more to life than these things!

Mortimer: What? Even the TV programs are boring. Most of them are reruns, anyway.

Mathilda: How long do you watch TV every day, Mortimer?

Mortimer: Oh, I don't know. Not very long, really.

Mathilda: Do you start watching it as soon as you get home from school?

Mortimer: Well, no. I get something to eat, first!

Mathilda: And I bet you watch TV while you eat your snack, don't you?

Mortimer: Yeah! How'd you know?

Mathilda: Then how long do you watch it?

Mortimer: Oh, until Mom calls me for supper around six.

Mathilda: Let's see, from four o'clock to six o'clock is two hours. Is that all you watch it?

Mortimer: Yeah, unless something good is on after supper.

Mathilda: And there's usually "something good" on, isn't there?

Mortimer: Yeah. Come to think of it. There is.

Mathilda: So you watch TV at least a couple more hours after supper?

Mortimer: Yeah. About that.

Mathilda: That's at least four hours a day you watch TV!

Mortimer: Yeah, I guess so. What's so bad about that?

Mathilda: How do you feel when you turn the TV off?

Mortimer: Tired, usually.

Mathilda: Why? You haven't done anything!

Mortimer: I don't know. But I feel tired all right!

Mathilda: And bored?

Mortimer: Yeah. I'm bored.

Mathilda: And lazy?

Mortimer: Well, tired. Hmmmm. Lazy, too, I guess.

Mathilda: Then you go to bed and get up and do the same things the next day?

Mortimer: Yeah.

Mathilda: Wow! No wonder you feel like you do! You make me feel tired and bored just listening to you!

Mortimer: See! There's nothing to do!

Mathilda: There's nothing to do!?! Oh, Mortimer. There are lots of things to do!

Mortimer: Like what?

Mathilda: Well, like reading your Bible.

Mortimer: I read my Bible. First thing in the morning.

Mathilda: Then what do you do with it?

Mortimer: I put it back on my dresser! What did you think I did with it?

Mathilda: No, I mean, what do you do with what you read?

Mortimer: Oh. I forget it, I guess. I get busy doing other things.

Mathilda: Mortimer, do you know why you're bored?

Mortimer: No, why?

Mathilda: Because you're thinking about yourself all the time. Even when you're watching TV you're pretending you're those guys doing all those things.

Mortimer: I'm not thinking about myself ALL the time!

Mathilda: Well, most of the time, then.

Mortimer: Yeah, I guess you're right. I *am* thinking about myself most of the time! So what? Doesn't everybody?

Mathilda: Everybody who's bored with life is, I guess. But I'm not. I think life is exciting!

Mortimer: So, why aren't you bored? What do you do that's so exciting?

Mathilda: Well, I think about God a lot, and about other people, and what God wants me to do with and for them.

Mortimer: That doesn't sound so exciting!

Mathilda: But it is! Thinking about myself wouldn't be, though. Did you know Jesus promised us abundant life?

Mortimer: Yeah. But my life sure isn't abundant!

Mathilda: How do you think Jesus means we can have it?

Mortimer: I don't know. How?

Mathilda: By accepting it!

Mortimer: Okay. I accept it! So what?

Mathilda: Oh, Mortimer. You know how you have to accept things from God!

Mortimer: By trusting Him for it?

Mathilda: Yes! By faith! And faith comes by reading and hearing the Bible!

Mortimer: So?

Mathilda: So, when I read the Bible, I pray God will give me what He wants me to have in it. Isn't that exciting? *God is actually talking to me!* And He has lots of things for me if I'll only receive them!

Mortimer: Well, I don't know. Like what?

Mathilda: That's what I'm talking about! *You* read the Bible and God talks to *you!*

Mortimer: No kidding! That *does* sound exciting! GOD TALKS TO ME! WOW!

Mathilda: Then when He talks to you, He tells you things He wants YOU to do!

Mortimer: Wow!

Mathilda: And when you do those things, He rewards you! But you have to do them first. And you won't know what the reward is until it happens! It's exciting every day to see what God has in store for me!

Mortimer: That *would* be exciting!

Mathilda: Why don't you try it? When you read your Bible, listen! Just think! God is talking to *you!* Listen to what He has to say to you!

Mortimer: Boy! I will!

Mathilda: And I bet He doesn't tell you to lead an old dull, boring life, either!

Mortimer: Wow! Me neither! Just to think God is talking to me is exciting! I think I'll go home right now and read my Bible.

(Mortimer and Mathilda leave the stage happily.)